Life
without
Lisa

BY RICHARD BALLO

⚓

A widowed father's compelling journey
through the rough seas of grief

Published By:

Quality of Life Publishing Co.
Naples, Florida

Quality of Life Publishing Co. specializes in clinical and grief support publications for hospices and other end-of-life care organizations. The mission-driven firm publishes *Quality of Life Matters*®, an end-of-life care periodical for physicians and other clinicians, and a line of gentle grief support books and booklets.

1-877-513-0099 (toll free in U.S. and Canada)
1-239-513-9907 (phone)
1-239-513-0088 (fax)

www.QoLpublishing.com

ISBN 0-9675532-4-5

Library of Congress Control Number: 2004095117

Cover photo © 2004 by Allan Wood

Richard Balk

DEDICATED TO LISA
for the life and love she gave me

...To the boys for giving me
a reason to keep on living

...To my family and friends
for standing by me

...And to hospice for helping me
heal and find hope

Contents

A Surreal Day

December 14, 1993. It's a sunny Tuesday afternoon in central Massachusetts as I drive west on Route 2 past I-495. The boys and I are making up dinosaur names for modern-day mammals like dogs, cats, and raccoons.

"What about cat-a-saur?" suggests Victor, my six-and-a-half-year-old son.

"That's good." I force a smile.

"Dog-a-saur!" yells Nick, my five-year-old.

The boys giggle, and it dawns on me that these kids are going to save me.

Save me from what?

Save me from the unknown future I now face. Early this morning, Lisa, my wife of eight years, died of cancer.

My thoughts travel backward. Several hours after leaving her bedside, I had woken up on the couch at my parents' house to see the boys standing there. I sat up, held out my arms, and wrapped them around the boys. "Your mom's gone," I said. The boys stood still, almost stiff in my arms. Did they comprehend what I had said? What did they feel at that moment? I was numb. Were they?

Because I've been a stay-at-home dad for five years and the boys' home-school teacher, I was usually able to tune into their feelings. Not today. Like me, they seemed totally void of emotion.

The silly dinosaur names flowing from the boys in the rear seat pull me back. I know I'll survive, but I don't begin to fathom how. I have faith in a power greater than I, and I know that life does go on. At other times in my life, when I felt crushed by emotions or physically challenged to the breaking point, I had persevered. My faith subtly reassured me that life would get better, and it did.

But this is different. The love of my life is gone. I feel that I need to be saved from what is coming my way. But I haven't a clue how.

⚓

Incredible. Every time a thought flashed through my mind about Lisa, that word popped up. Not only was she an inventor and a successful entrepreneur, she was also the sensitive, affectionate mother of our two precious boys. The company she founded secured our financial future together and that of our children. This vibrant woman who had just died at age 38 had overwhelmed me since the first time I looked into her eyes 12 years ago. From that moment on, she was the only woman I ever wanted to be with. And I'd never again be with her on earth. I can't begin to comprehend that reality.

⚓

My attention returns to the road, but only for an instant. I recall reading that when tragic events happen, the body and mind go into shock. Then reality sets in and grieving takes place. This numbness I am feeling must be a result of shock. When will the tidal wave of grief come crashing down? How will I soothe my children's pain while dealing with my own? At this point just hours after Lisa's death, I don't know how grief will affect my everyday life, except to know that it will be affected.

But here in the car, I can't be sure of anything beyond the next mile marker. I've driven Route 2 thousands of times since first meeting Lisa, yet today I feel like I am traveling it for the first time.

Last evening, a wise friend and counselor told me to be gentle with myself, that it could take me five years to come to terms with the loss of my soulmate. Five years to recover? How can that be? I also had read that the stages of grief take a year. In the life of five- and six-year-olds, a year could seem like eternity. It already seems like forever to me.

I know the way home by heart, but what is home? If "home is where the heart is," then I don't have a home. The only reason I know I have a heart is that I can feel the relentless pounding in my chest. However, my feelings and passions have left me.

What is waiting for me at home now? An assembly of people, including Carl, my 78-year-old widowed father-in-law; Bonda, Lisa's older sister; Julia, our six-month-old, yet-to-be-adopted daughter; Virginie, our 24-year-old nanny; Lisa's cousin Cheryl; and Cheryl's husband Don.

⚓

On November 1st, our family was supposed to board Amtrak's auto train to Florida to start living in the house we'd recently purchased. We'd made arrangements for Cheryl and Don to act as caretakers of our Massachusetts house during the ten-month period we'd reside in Florida. But Lisa entered the hospital in early October and was still there after three weeks, causing us to cancel the trip to Florida. Cheryl and Don remained with us, since they had nowhere else to live. I accepted that Lisa needed to stay in the hospital without questioning *why* she was still there. She promised me that everything would be all right. She always kept her promises, didn't she?

⚓

When the boys and I arrive home, the house is quiet, even with everyone in it. I can't look at my father-in-law. He can't look at me. We both know it would be too painful right now to acknowledge that the light of our lives — our cherished Lisa — is gone.

The kids want to play, so Virginie keeps them busy. Having arrived from France less than a month ago, our nanny knew Lisa only as someone in a hospital bed. She doesn't know what to say to us. It's okay. I understand.

With sad faces, Cheryl and Don try to be supportive but don't know what to do or say. Lisa's sister sits on the screened porch, smoking cigarettes. Carl retreats to his apartment, which is connected to the house.

Because I don't know what to do with myself, I wander around the first floor of the house. The boxes are still stacked in the front foyer from our most recent remodeling project. In the den, toy trucks and blocks litter the floor. The wallpaper is starting to peel in the TV room. The living room needs to be cleaned up. I can't bear to look at the collage of happy family pictures I had assembled and hung through our years together. The kitchen, as usual, needs to be straightened. I don't know where the time goes. The day slides away into the dark, cold December night.

I bring the kids upstairs for bed. I carry Julia to her bedroom and lay her gently into the same crib the boys slept in when they were babies. She is the baby we had hoped to adopt and call our daughter. I kiss my finger and softly place it on her sleepy head. As if in a dream, I walk down the hall to the boys' bedroom.

I sit on the bed with each of the boys and begin to talk about the day.

"I never said goodbye," Victor admits in a quiet voice.

"When I called you from the hospital, I held the phone to Mom's ear so you could say something."

"I didn't say anything."

I'm somewhat irritated that Victor didn't seize that moment, but I search to find a loving reply. After all, he's just a little kid who's lost his mother. My heart aches for him. "It's okay, Victor," I whisper as I hold him close. My tears fall onto his blondish brown hair and I'm reminded of how much he looks like Lisa. Similar color hair, same pale blue eyes.

Nick jumps onto my lap and wraps his arms around my neck. The three of us cling to each other. No one wants to let go.

"You know, you can talk to Mom any time," I reassure the boys, "because I believe her spirit is still alive, and she will know it's you."

We sit in silence — three weary swimmers adrift in a sea of shock and grief.

"I'll see you in the morning. I love you." I carry Nick to his bed.

"What are we doing tomorrow?" asks Nick.

"I don't know." I sigh. "But I know we'll be together."

I give Nick an extra long hug. He loves his hugs.

As I stand at their bedroom door, I begin to sing the lullaby Lisa and I routinely sang to the boys at bedtime. It was a favorite of hers, written by the Beatles. "Now it's time to say good night. Good night. Sleep tight. Now the sun turns out his light. Good night. Sleep tight." My voice cracks and I can't finish the first stanza. The boys — alone now with their own thoughts and feelings on this tragic night — don't even seem to notice. I doubt I will ever be able to sing that song again.

Wearily, I amble down the hall past the bathroom and stairs into my room. I get ready for bed and crawl under the covers alone, just as I have done for the past two months. Yet this night is different. The floodgates open wide, and gut-wrenching tears drench my pillow.

The difference tonight is that hope has died. The hope that she would survive another stay in the hospital is dead. The hope that we would have more time together is dead. The belief in her invincibility is dead. The hope of a married life lived until old age is dead. I feel like I'm drowning in an ocean of tears. My entire being is filled with an aching I've never known before.

I wish I were dead.

2

Grim Reality

December 15, 1993. Daylight arrives. I have survived. Why am I alive and Lisa dead? I stretch my arms across the bed, hoping that maybe it was all a nightmare and if I reach far enough I'll feel the softness of Lisa beside me. But I am alone.

I hear thumping on the stairs. The boys must be up and running around. Is Julia awake yet? Just as I'm about to roll out of bed to check on her, I hear Virginie's muffled voice down the hall. She has everything under control.

I pull the covers up over my head and try to hide from reality. I don't want to think about the burial details, but I know I must. I force myself out of bed to shower, dress, and go downstairs.

Lisa's father and I drive to the cemetery and meet with the caretaker. We walk to the area where plots are available. On the south side of the road are two-person plots, and on the north side are four-person plots.

I know Carl plans to be buried in another cemetery with his late wife and late son. I don't think of the boys as being ready for a plot, and I know I'm not ready for one, yet I pick the two-person plot because it has a view of the shopping mall. Lisa liked to shop, so it seems fitting that she should have a view of the mall. That thought brings a slight smile to my lips.

Our next stop is the funeral home. Richardson's is situated in an older house with large rooms and a veranda that sweeps around the front. Carl and I sit in the small office and tell Mr. Richardson Lisa's biographical information, which he needs for the funeral forms and newspaper obituary.

Here I am telling this stranger Lisa's vital information. It seems I could be talking about a car or a watermelon instead of my wife. I am completely vacant inside: cold, emotionless, capable of only single-syllable words. I am simply taking care of business.

"Is there anything special you would like at the burial?" Mr. Richardson asks.

"Yes," I respond. "After the casket has been lowered, I want to throw a handful of dirt into the grave."

"That will be fine." He makes a note of my request.

Many years ago when I was single, a friend died in a scuba-diving accident. A group of his friends, including me, threw dirt into the grave as a farewell to him, and this helped soothe our grief. For me, this gesture, the throwing of the dirt, symbolizes closure, the final goodbye.

We set tomorrow, Thursday afternoon, as the time for a family viewing of the body. The public viewing will be held on Thursday and Friday evenings. Now it is time to choose a casket. We head into the basement, which has been made into a display room for coffins. If Mr. Richardson tells me prices, I don't hear them. The caskets are all open to showcase the colors inside and out. They have a nice finish to them, I think, as I run my hand over the smooth wood surface. I see a casket the color of cherry wood.

"I'll take this one," I state with conviction.

"Why that model?" asks Carl.

"It's the color Lisa had selected for the kitchen cabinets." It makes sense to me and, for a moment, I picture her admiring our new kitchen.

When we remodeled the old kitchen, she wanted cherry-colored kitchen cabinets. We searched and couldn't find cabinets in the color or style she wanted, so I decided to make them. From the manufacturer, I bought a five-gallon pail of cherry stain to use with the cherry veneer. Lisa loved the cabinets and thanked me again and again for all my hard work and craftsmanship. It didn't matter to me what color the cabinets were; it mattered that she was happy.

⚓

We purchase the cherry-colored casket.

We arrive home, and I greet all the kids. Carl announces he's going to lie down for a nap. I ask Virginie to watch Julia while Victor, Nicholas, and I go out.

⚓

The boys and I are going shopping for a headstone. At the age of 39, I should not be shopping for a headstone. The boys should not be shopping for a headstone at the tender ages of five and six. I want the boys to be part of the process because we are a family, we do things together, and they need to feel involved. She is their mother, and they never told her goodbye.

On Main Street in Leominster, adjacent to the cemetery, is Hathaway Memorials. The blue sky belies our somber mission on this clear, cold day. I shiver as a gust of wind blows the chilly December air. Shopping for a headstone reminds me of shopping for a car; you try to decide on the perfect combination of color and looks. I stroll among the stones without much interest. No stone is right for Lisa. I know the boys will find a headstone that suits their mother.

I watch the boys as they search each row of carved stones. "How about this one?" Nick asks, pointing to a light pink stone with a carving of a heart and Jesus.

"That's a nice one, but let's keep looking," I respond. Lisa was spiritual but not very religious. We did go to church, and the boys attended Sunday School, but we didn't read the Bible every night.

We walk some more. "How about this one?" suggests Victor.

We stand before a polished black granite stone. Etched on its surface is a lighthouse on a rocky shore, waves crashing onto the rocks.

"Mom liked the ocean," Victor states matter-of-factly.

I nod. The lighthouse reminds me that Lisa was such a bright beacon of light to me and to others. "What do you think, Nick?"

Nick remains quiet. "It's all right," he acquiesces without enthusiasm.

"Is it just 'all right' or is it good?" I ask Nick.

"It's good."

"Then this is the one we'll take."

We enter the small business office and fill out the forms. We decide the name "Ballo" will be etched on the front of the headstone, to the right of the lighthouse. Lisa's full maiden name, "Melissa C. Johnson," and the dates of her birth and death will appear on the back.

"Do you want any special saying on it?" the salesman asks.

I pause for a moment because I'm not prepared for the question. What would be appropriate? Then I think of a favorite drawing that Lisa kept at home. It's a picture of a wood stork with a frog in its mouth. The bird is trying to swallow the frog, but the frog has its hands wrapped around the bird's throat to prevent it from being swallowed. The caption reads, "Don't ever give up."

That's the saying I choose to be etched under her name, for she never gave up her fight for life. She tried traditional medicine and non-traditional therapies to combat the cancer that had already spread by the time she was diagnosed with a malignant tumor. All methods helped extend her life, but in the end, they failed to save her.

As we leave the office, the middle-aged owner of Hathaway Memorials appears. "I lost my wife 15 years ago," he offers. "Every now and then, when I think of her, I feel the pain again. But it's bearable now."

I stare at him. Lisa's been gone only one day, and this man is trying to tell me that — with time — everything will be okay again?

My feet quickly carry me to the car, and the boys ask me why I'm in a hurry. I have no answer for them.

⚓

Thursday morning, the boys, Carl, and I stand in the kitchen, ready to travel to the funeral home for the private viewing. Descending the stairs with her suitcase in hand is Bonda, Lisa's older sister and Carl's only surviving child.

To my utter shock, Bonda announces, "I don't do wakes and funerals. I'm going back home to California." With that, she turns and walks out the door.

How can she leave her father at this time? The man lost his only son in Vietnam, his wife died 13 years ago, and now he is about to bury his youngest daughter. The man has lost almost his whole family, and now his last remaining child is deserting him?

I think I hear her crying as she closes the door.

I don't understand. If she didn't want to attend the wake, she could have stayed at the house and helped us with any number of tasks. She could provide support for Carl and get some support for herself. But she abandons all of us.

I can't bear to look at Carl. Families stay together and help each other, don't they? Bonda's abrupt departure must be almost as painful for Carl as Lisa's death.

⚓

Carl, the boys, and I arrive at the funeral home to view the body. The boys accompany me into the small parlor off to the left of the entryway. Lisa's body is in the coffin, and the lid is open. The boys and I approach the casket and look at her body.

She is wearing her red-and-black business dress. Her wavy hair is in place, but not exactly as she wore it. Her face is a grayish color. I can't accept that I'm looking at her, and she isn't alive. All feeling has abandoned me and I gaze upon her in a stupor.

"Is she sleeping?" asks Nick, his five-year-old mind striving to understand.

"No, her spirit has left her body," I calmly explain. "It's Mom's body, but it isn't Mom anymore."

Nick reaches out and touches her arm, pushing at it, trying to tell if she is real or some kind of bizarre life-size doll. Why is his mother there but not warm and soft like before?

I watch his hand as he touches her. I'm fascinated — and horrified — that he has reached out to touch her, but I don't say a word. I try to put myself in his shoes, yet know that I would never think of touching a dead body lying in a casket. Not even my dear Lisa's.

⚓

My mind wanders back to two days ago. It is half past midnight on Tuesday, December 14. Gail, who was Lisa's maid-of-honor, and I wait for the doctor to arrive and make the death pronouncement. I don't want or need to hear those final words, but hospital policy dictates that I be forced to hear them. What harsh, insensitive rules, I think, but I'm powerless to utter that objection.

Gail sits in the chair opposite me and stares into the distance. Judy, another friend and nurse, arrives to keep me company, too. I glance at them briefly, and I reluctantly acknowledge the doctor. Mostly my eyes study the floor so I can avoid having to look at people who are looking at me or my dead wife.

I am the last to leave. I bend over to give Lisa one final kiss. My lips touch her cheek, and I am startled — and shocked — by how cold her body has become in less than an hour. For 12 years she has always been warm to my touch, and I assumed she would always be warm to me.

It was the last time I touched her.

⚓

Thursday evening, the kids stay home while Carl and I drive to the funeral home for the wake. I greet friends and family and thank them for coming. It really is good to see everyone, even though some look lost. Several of our closest friends notice Bonda is missing. All I can say is that she left.

The kids are asleep when I arrive home. I go to my room and change for bed. Then I open Lisa's dresser drawers and touch all the underwear, pajamas, sweaters, and scarves. I look at the items on top of the dresser: hair brushes, jewelry box, pictures, cigarette lighter, coins, pens, Chanel No. 5 perfume, knickknacks with sayings on them, and various tubes of lipstick.

I take the small bottle of Chanel No. 5 perfume, open it, and inhale a flood of memories. For an instant, I feel calm and loved. Then a sense of loneliness envelops me.

I enter the closet and hug her clothes. Her scent is here, her presence is here, and I want her to be in my arms again, but all I can hold are her clothes. I slide Lisa's soft pullover jersey off the hanger, fold it, and take it to bed with me. Like an infant with its blankie, hugging the jersey to my chest comforts me.

⚓

I'm vaguely aware that neighbors have been stopping by to drop off casseroles and other food dishes. I make a mental note to find out later who brought us what so I can thank them for their thoughtfulness. If Lisa were here, she'd be keeping a notepad handy to keep track of details like this so she could send one of her cheery thank you notes.

The second night of the wake passes by like a slow-motion movie. I've rehearsed all my lines already and simply act out my role. The funeral director stays near so he can replenish my supply of dry tissues, which I often share with whoever is offering me their condolences.

The day of the funeral I ask the boys if they want to go. They decide to stay home with Virginie and Julia. I call my friend, Patty, a mom from the play group I used to attend with the boys. She agrees to drive Victor, Nick, Virginie, and Julia to the park.

⚓

The funeral service is about to begin at Pilgrim Congregational Church. This is the church where Lisa and I were married almost eight years ago. It is also the church where the boys were baptized and attended Sunday School classes.

I sit near the front with my sister Stephanie on my left. I want to turn around to see who is here, but I don't. I am tired of looking at the casket and exhausted from all the preparations. I watch as the minister who married us addresses the congregation; then the new minister speaks. Our best friend, Sue, was going to deliver a eulogy, but she lost her voice the day before.

I am struck by the symbolism of Sue losing her voice the same week Lisa's voice has been silenced forever. Sue and Lisa shared pain. If Lisa had backaches, Sue would feel them. They were not only close friends, but Sue has worked with Lisa at her company for 12 years and has been running the business during Lisa's illness. Sue's oldest daughter, Erica, reads the piece that Sue had written.

The service is all very nice. Everything everyone says is nice. I can't think beyond things being "nice" because I can't accept that I am here sitting in a pew, inhaling and exhaling, and Lisa is lying dead in that cherry-colored coffin.

This is insane. This is not right. I rock slightly back and forth in the pew until I feel a hand on my shoulder. It's my sister signaling it's time to go. I seem to have gained weight during the service, for it is difficult to stand. My feet feel like lead weights as my sister holds my arm. We make our way out of the church and into the limousine.

At Evergreen Cemetery, I see that a temporary canvas roof has been erected over the gravesite. People are already surrounding the casket when I exit the limousine. I stumble over to the inner ring of people and face the casket. I look around at all the friends and family standing there. Mrs. Niemi, our friend and spiritual counselor, is by my side. She and a few others closest to the gravesite hold my arms as the ministers intone their prayers for the dead.

Then it's over.

No one moves.

No one breathes a word.

The silence wraps us together in a blanket of finality. We don't want to leave behind this beautiful, vibrant woman, this incredible person who has touched us all.

I have to do something or I am going to explode.

"On the count of three, would you all join me in a scream?" my voice rolls out. I count, "One. Two. Three."

I scream. The air fills with one, huge voice screaming in agony. Mine and everyone else's.

My body sags. I stamp my right foot so hard against the cold ground that I hurt my ankle.

Someone leads me back to the limo. Wait a minute. I planned to throw dirt on the grave. Why am I being led back to the car? I can't speak; I can only follow directions. I sit in the car and watch everyone move away slowly. The funeral director comes over and opens my door.

"You can throw the dirt now," he says.

He didn't forget. I walk to the gravesite and bend down at the edge of the open grave. I reach for the dirt, but it is frozen. I claw angrily at the lifeless dirt until I have a handful. I stand and stretch my arm over the gaping hole.

My hand doesn't open. I stare at my hand. "Open, dammit," I silently command, yet my hand still won't open. My hand doesn't want to let go. I concentrate, mustering all my emotional strength. I strain my arm muscles. Finally my hand opens, and the dirt thuds onto her coffin. I limp back to the limo and slump into the back seat.

Opening my hand should have been such a simple, physical act, but after Lisa's death, I find that even simple, everyday acts are monumentally difficult. I will come to learn this is normal, but right then, I knew nothing about the grieving process. Only that it hurts like hell.

⚓

The night Lisa died, after everyone left, it was time for me to say goodbye and leave Lisa's hospital room for the last time. It should have been simple to walk through the door. When I reached the door, I turned back and looked at her. And found I couldn't move.

I leaned against the doorjamb. How could I leave her? I've been at her side in health and in sickness. Now I was expected to just walk out and leave her lying in the hospital bed? The rational part of me knew she was dead and nothing I could do would change that, but she is — was — my wife.

It took all my willpower to find the strength in my legs to finally turn my back on her and walk out the door.

⚓

After the funeral, we all arrive back at our house. Adults are talking, eating, and milling about, while kids romp around in the backyard with Virginie. I have been to receptions after funerals, so I know what to expect, but this reception is different. After most of the people leave, I wander into the living room and lie down on the couch. My friends Allan, Ted, and Jean join me. They ask about Bonda.

"She left," I say, telling them the whole story.

They shake their heads in disbelief. They clearly don't understand any more than I do why Bonda didn't stay.

3

Going Through the Motions

December 18, 1993. "This is not an easy time," I say to Virginie, stating the obvious as we sit in the living room. Her short blond hair is in sharp contrast to her black sweater. She looks vulnerable and small.

"You came into the middle of this. If you don't want to stay, I will understand."

Blessedly, she replies without hesitation in her French accent, "I will stay."

Relieved, I thank her and retreat to my room.

⚓

It was Lisa's idea that we hire a nanny. She wanted me — the stay-at-home dad and home-school teacher — to have time to devote to my freelance writing career. Besides, Lisa argued, not only would the nanny be helping *us,* we would be helping *her* by hiring a nanny from Europe who wouldn't otherwise have the opportunity to work in America.

⚓

I call Denise in Italy. She had been our nanny for the last year, but she had to leave a month before Lisa died. In English and broken Italian, I tell her that Lisa has died. I hear Denise cry. The death of a loved one is hard to discuss in any language. Saying that Lisa is dead makes it real in my mind. If I say it, it must be true. I don't want it to be true, but I have to say it, anyway.

⚓

It is now seven days before Christmas. Where is my mind? I eat, but I never think of food until my stomach growls. I play with the kids or sit with them when necessary, but my mind is completely blank, and I feel like I'm just going through the motions of being a father. I feed Julia, change her diaper, and hold her. She smiles at me, and I smile back, not so much for joy but for the sake of doing something right.

⚓

I think of Florida. Eleven months ago, Lisa and her business partners decided to move their prospering medical device company, M.C. Johnson Co., to Naples, Florida. As a freelance technical writer, I was flexible to make the move, too, even though I would have preferred to stay in Massachusetts. We bought our Naples house in June and furnished it in July. In October, my brother Ed drove to Florida in my car filled with a load of my stuff. Lisa had wanted to wait to send her belongings until she was feeling better. We registered the kids as being home-schooled.

Early in November we cancelled plans to take the auto train to Florida because Lisa was admitted to the hospital. We planned to be in Naples for Thanksgiving to celebrate with our close friends Sue and Joe, but we had to cancel that, too. As Lisa's health deteriorated, the date for leaving Massachusetts kept getting pushed further back.

Even though I knew she needed treatment for cancer, I

had hoped to fly Lisa to Florida, where she could be cared for in our new home. I received information from the hospital on air transportation. It was expensive, but it was something we could manage. I called homecare companies in Naples to inquire about providing services in the house, such as a hospital bed. Then her doctor said that her health was so poor it would be dangerous to move her. All hope for seeing Lisa in our new Florida home was dashed.

⚓

Now, on this frigid December day, the only thought I can hold in my head is that we had decided as a family to move to Naples, where we would live for most of the year, returning to Massachusetts each summer. This was Lisa's dream, and I feel compelled to carry out her plans. I gather Victor, Nick, Carl, Virginie, and my parents, who have come to stay with us during the holidays, so I can make an announcement: "We're going to Florida." I make flight plans for January 14.

⚓

There are 14 of us in the house for Christmas: my mom and dad, sister, two brothers, sister-in-law, Cheryl and Don, Carl, Virginie, Julia, the two boys, and me. We want to be together on Christmas morning so we can see the kids open their presents.

Our turn-of-the-century house with its five bedrooms, three-and-a-half stories, and 5,000 square feet of living area is comfortable and accommodating. It's a place where we hang our coats and hats, where the kids can feel free to run around, and where the kids' toys are scattered across the floor. The huge living room with three sofas doubles as a sleeping area for some of our holiday guests.

On Christmas Day, we all gather in the living room to open presents. Julia is wearing an adorable green Christmas dress and bonnet.

As happens with most six-month-olds, all the gifts she receives end up in her mouth.

The boys climb in and out of the battery-operated riding jeep their uncles and aunt have given them. The nurses at Emerson Hospital sent them a Santa plate and several small toys. I bought them a few things before Lisa died. They seem satisfied.

There are presents for me this Christmas morning, but the only gift I want is my life with Lisa.

"Thank you," I say automatically, as I open each package. The gifts could be dog crap, and I would say thank you. I just don't care. For me there is no joy, just an emptiness that can't be filled, and a chasm that can't be forded.

After the gift-opening, I drag myself upstairs to our bedroom. I sit cross-legged on the carpet and look at the three paper shopping bags I brought home from the hospital. I gently remove Lisa's belongings and look at each piece of clothing, remembering where it came from and when Lisa used or wore it. Price tags dangle from the tropical clothing I had bought her for our new Florida life.

I put the clothing in her dresser and the cards into a box.

"Merry Christmas," I say. The room doesn't reply.

Later in the afternoon we bundle up the kids and take them outside with their new jeep. The ground is blanketed with three inches of freshly fallen snow, and the jeep makes tracks as the boys trek across the driveway and frozen lawn. I take videos of them. Nick is hugging a teddy bear as his brother drives him around the yard. They crash into the maple tree and laugh. I am struck by how resilient young children can be during times of tragedy. The smiles on Victor's and Nick's faces are as huge and genuine as ever. No one would ever guess these boys had just lost their mother.

⚓

The days after Christmas disappear. Grief overwhelms me. I don't want to get out of bed. I'm not hungry. I don't want to see anyone, and I have nothing to say, anyway. I am breathing, and Lisa isn't. I am alive, and Lisa isn't. I am ashamed. I am ashamed that she is dead, and I am still alive. What more could I have done to save her? I don't know enough about grief to realize that this guilt is the first step down the road toward healing.

The days all seem the same. Virginie plays with the boys. I help with Julia. It snows, and I stay indoors. Then, I answer the phone one day and find myself forced to make some decisions.

"Hi, Rich, this is Mary at the adoption center. We need to reassure the agency that things will be all right with the adoption," she explains. "They want to know that you are going through with it and that you have female role models for Julia."

"Uh huh," I reply.

"You need to book a flight on the 31st to join me as we meet with the birth mother's family and the adoption agency."

"Okay," I say, as I cling to one-word sentences.

We book the flight for Carl, my mother, and myself. December 31st arrives, and we all climb aboard the plane. As the plane lands, I turn to Mary and ask her for the tenth time, "Why are we here?"

"To let them know that Julia will be cared for and brought up right, even though Lisa has died."

We arrive at our destination, and the next morning find ourselves sitting across the table from the 15-year-old birth mother, her mother, and the adoption agency personnel. It is New Year's Day, and it has been six months since Lisa, the boys, our previous nanny Denise, and I traveled across the country to the blazing southwestern United States to meet these people and bring home newborn Julia.

⚓

Lisa wanted four children, but the cancer prevented her from having any more after Victor and Nicholas. That's when we started to visit adoption agencies. We found one that would accept us even though Lisa had cancer, as long as I stayed healthy and capable.

Back in July, Lisa and I received notice that a baby had been born, and if we wanted her, we would need to travel immediately. Lisa made the arrangements, and the boys, Denise, and I flew out west for an undetermined length of time, since we didn't know how long the process would take. It was an open adoption in which the birth parents could meet us and know where their child was going.

We met the teenaged birth mom and birth dad, along with their parents. The birth mother and father had been going together at one point, but were now split up. The birth mother told us she wanted a better future for her daughter than she could provide. She seemed glad to know we could give her baby a loving home and a solid start in life.

The next day we went to the hospital and picked up the four-day-old baby girl, whom we named Julia. We stayed in the area for a week before we got on a plane and headed home. Julia was ten days old when she took her first airplane flight.

⚓

That was six months ago. Today at the adoption agency, we say yes, the adoption is still going through. The female role models are my mother, our nanny Virginie, and my sister. We report that Grandpa Carl also lives with us to help with the children.

The next day we leave the heat of winter in the southwest and return to the snow of central Massachusetts.

⚓

On the evening of January 13, the night before we are to leave for Florida, I wander through the house. I notice water dripping into the living room along the ceiling beam that separates the living room from the dining room. I go directly upstairs into the boys' room and find water seeping from the window onto the floor. I check the attic above the boys' room and find it dry. I go back to the boys' room and crawl out the window onto the snow-covered living room roof. Ice has formed along the whole edge of the roof, causing water to back up into the house. I run to the basement, grab a crow bar, and head out onto the roof.

"Be careful out there," Carl urges.

Be careful? Of course I'm going to be careful. What does he think I'm going to do? Jump off? Hit myself on the head? I want to break the ice, not kill myself. I crawl out the window.

"I don't need this," I yell, as I whack away at the ice. Why did this have to happen now? We're scheduled to leave for sunny Florida in a matter of hours. This is the first time in nine years ice has built up and forced water to back up into the house. I attack the ice until I see bits of shingle fly off the roof. "Just get me out of here," I scream, as I climb back into the house.

Relocation

January 1994. It is a warm, sunny day as our large family strolls off the plane at Southwest Regional Airport in Fort Myers, Florida. One by one my mom, dad, Carl, Virginie (who is holding Julia), Victor, Nicholas, and I fold ourselves inside an airport shuttle van. Forty minutes later, we arrive at our home in Naples.

I'm glad to be out of the cold. I think I would have gone bonkers had I stayed stuck in the house up north.

⚓

When Lisa first decided to relocate her business to Florida, I didn't want to leave Massachusetts. But for 12 years, I had gone wherever Lisa went.

"If we're going to be in Florida, we should be near the beach," I remember Lisa saying.

"We can get a bigger house inland," I countered.

She shook her head. "Florida is the beach. That's why people move there."

When we began to search for a house in Naples, we looked at one property on the Gulf of Mexico and many more within walking distance of the beach. We picked an older, ranch-styled house because it was a mere five-minute walk to the beach and had ample room for our extended family.

⚓

The 40-year-old house is a three-bedroom split floor plan with a living room/dining room combination running from front to back, separating the master bedroom from the other two bedrooms. Lisa and I especially liked the fact that there was a 525-square-foot recreation room, large enough to convert, someday, into two additional bedrooms.

Sleeping arrangements had been predetermined. Carl, who is 78 years old, an amputee below the right knee, and hard of hearing, takes the master bedroom with its small private bath. My parents move into the large bedroom on the left side of the house, and Virginie takes the room next to my parents. The two boys, Julia, and I settle into the recreation room. This room — our room — has a bar at one end, dark paneling, and a low ceiling. It could double as a cave.

When I want peace and quiet, I have to leave the house.

The saving grace is the weather. It's in the 70's during the day. It is great not to have to put on multiple layers of clothing just to go outside.

⚓

Two days following our arrival, the boys and I are outside, wearing short-sleeved shirts — hard to believe it's January — and throwing a baseball around when a UPS truck pulls up.

"Richard Ballo?" asks the driver.

"Yes."

"Sign here."

I sign the pad, and he hands over a Next Day Letter envelope.

This is curious. I've been in Florida two days, and someone has found me. I open the envelope and remove the contents. My smile fades.

It's a letter from Lisa's insurance company with the death benefit check. Great. It's a concrete reminder of the indisputable fact that Lisa is gone and isn't coming back. I stuff the check and letter back into the envelope.

Suddenly I am very tired. I toss the ball to Victor and create an excuse to take time out from our game. I go inside and lie down on my bed.

⚓

This same kind of shock hit me 12 hours after Lisa died. The boys and I left my mom's house, and I took them back to the hospital so they could meet with Kay, the counselor for kids who are sick or whose parents are seriously ill or dying. While the boys talked to Kay, I went to the hospital wing where Lisa died. I visited the nurses' station and thanked them for all their help. Then I turned and walked over to Lisa's private room.

For two months, this room had been a big part of my life, and I just wanted to see it again. Knowing better, I hoped Lisa was still there, still alive. I approached the doorway, and as I stepped closer, I panicked. There was someone alive and in the room, but it wasn't Lisa. I quickly turned away and headed down the hallway and off the floor, my heart pounding all the way.

Of course there would be someone there, I told myself. It's a hospital. It's a business. But how could they get some-one in there so quickly? It had been less than a day. I sat in the lobby and stared at the ceiling. Nothing is the same, I thought. Nothing in my life would ever be the same.

⚓

After a short nap, I realize I am desperate to find someone to help me from sinking further into the abyss of grief, so I call hospice. A social worker from Emerson Hospital in Massachusetts explained to me that most community hospice organizations offer bereavement groups for adults, as well as support groups for grieving children, even when the dying patient wasn't cared for by hospice. Following a brief telephone conversation with the hospice grief counselor at Hospice of Naples, I make plans to attend the evening adult grief support meetings and for the boys to attend a children's group, which is held at a local public school.

Although I have no clue what these bereavement meetings might entail and whether the three of us can withstand having to talk about our feelings, I visualize the grief counselors throwing each of us a rescue rope so we won't drown in our tears and fears.

⚓

My parents and Carl return from a shopping trip with two televisions, one for Carl and one for everyone else. Carl loves to watch TV as much as he loves to read newspapers. Carl bought two TV stands, too. They have to be assembled, so I have a job to do.

Ready to tackle an easy manual task, I set up shop in the recreation room and begin fitting screws into the predrilled holes of wood-veneered fiberboard. While balancing the pieces and positioning the screws, I call over my shoulder to ask Lisa for the screwdriver. Dammit! I've forgotten she isn't here and that I've lost her. Dammit! On a day like today she would have been sitting near me because we loved doing ordinary household tasks together. We always chattered happily when doing projects around the house. But she wasn't here for today's project, and she's never going to be here again.

My breathing becomes faster and deeper as I fight with the emotions that are crawling up my throat. This is crazy. I'm going to burst. I drop the sections of the stand.

"I'm going to the beach," I yell out as I leave the house. I turn right and follow the road a couple blocks to the beach. I walk to the small jetty and sit on top of the rocks.

I stare at the large silver and gray waves. Lisa liked being near the water. She said it brought her peace and helped put things in perspective. But the beauty of the calm waters of the Gulf of Mexico cannot put her death in perspective for me. Why did she have to die? I don't care about the medical reasons; I know what they were. But why? What was the reason she died and left me and the kids? I beseech God, or the powers that be, to give me an answer as to why they took her. She is needed here. The boys need her. I need her. I want an answer.

I don't get one.

I hold my head in my hands and stare at the wet rocks below my feet. My foundation — my rock — has crumbled and I'm floundering. This life stinks. I can't do simple things without breaking down. I'm a mess, and I'm angry with the woman I love because she died and left me. She changed my whole life when I met her, and she changed my life again when she left me. I know that she can't come back, but I'm living in a new state and now I have three kids instead of two. Plus, I have to deal with her father directly without her intervention and in addition, I must deal with her business as well as coordinate tasks for our European nanny. I can manage all that, and yet I can't put a stupid television stand together without breaking down and crying!

⚓

The gulf waves continue to roll. My breathing slows to normal. I get up and stroll back to the house.

I glare at the television stand. It's still in pieces. No one has put it together. No one has helped me. It's all left up to me. Everything is up to me.

I feel like I have been hit on the head with a sledgehammer, yet I am supposed to act like nothing has happened and somehow keep on living a normal life.

Grief Support

January 1994. One month without Lisa. "I'm going to the grief support meeting at hospice," I announce one evening.

"Don't worry about the kids," my mom answers. "They'll be fine."

I'm grateful to have such a caring and supportive mother.

I arrive at Hospice of Naples. I find the meeting room for the bereavement group, fill out a nametag, and take a seat in the circle of chairs. There are about 20 people in the circle, and most of them are older than I am. Two women appear to be close to my age, but the rest of the group members look to be in their sixties and seventies.

"My name is Ms. Susan, the facilitator here," the grief counselor begins in a gentle voice. "We'd like you to fill out the login form that's going around so we know something about you. Then we'll start by introducing ourselves." The form has a place for my name, the name of my deceased loved one, that person's relationship to me and date of death.

It's my turn to speak. "My name is Rich. My wife died of cancer, and I have three kids."

When the introductions are finished, the discussion begins. We talk of coping, taking on new roles, and redefining ourselves without our loved ones by our side. Ms. Susan tells us that if we find ourselves crying uncontrollably at times, that's perfectly normal. "It's okay to cry," she says. "Tears help let the pain out."

I don't contribute anything to the session. I'm afraid to open my mouth because if I begin talking, I'll start crying, and I'm embarrassed to cry. The meeting is an hour long. People tell stories about their loss. I feel myself sinking deeper and deeper into the raw, tormenting emotions of life without Lisa. I feel everyone's pain, and I want to scream. I want to get out of the room. Despair wells up inside me, and it threatens to burst from me.

When the meeting ends, I head straight for Lisa's car, which she had nicknamed Big Blue. I open the door, slide into the driver's seat, lock the door, let the anguish overwhelm me, and start sobbing. How will I survive this? How will I make it through?

At my core, I know I must continue to attend these grief support meetings — as tortuous as they seem — if I want to heal my heart and live again. I owe it to myself and to the kids. I miss Lisa so much. Right now I have to let the tears and the pain flow out. Didn't the grief counselor just tell me it was okay — even good — to cry?

When I stop crying and dry my eyes, I start Big Blue and drive home.

⚓

Today I am meeting with a pediatrician to evaluate whether or not she's the right one for the kids. This is the type of responsibility Lisa and I always shared, so making a decision like this on my own is new to me. The doctor and I talk, and I decide I'd like her to become our new pediatrician.

In the waiting room, I start to fill in the paperwork for the three kids. I stop at the line for mother's name. Do I put down Lisa's name even though she is dead? What about Julia's parents' names? I just put my name down for Julia. For the boys, I fill in Lisa's name and write "deceased." It seems to take forever to fill out the boys' forms because I am forced to remember that their mother is dead. I hand the papers to the office manager and leave.

I start the car and then turn it off. Finding a doctor for the kids without Lisa to help me turns out to be a lonely, stressful experience. Because she was a nurse, I depended on her to take the lead in finding the best doctors for our family. I have to adjust and learn to do what she would have done.

I don't feel like going home. I know when I get home the kids will be all over me. They'll want my undivided attention. Right now I have to nurture myself. I have to have something for me. I head over to the local shopping center and buy some vitamins. I retreat into a bike shop to look around. I buy a bicycle pump and lock. I still don't want to go home, so I window-shop until I feel settled enough to face my family.

I used to think in terms of "our" family. Now, it's only mine. Another brutal reminder.

⚓

The grapefruit tree in the backyard is so heavily laden with fruit that the branches sag onto the flat roof over the rec room. I climb out on the roof, bag dozens of fruit, and begin trimming the branches.

Then Carl is the bearer of bad tidings when he yells up to me that we've run out of hot water. In addition, my father tells me he noticed that the ground is wet on the far side of the driveway. I had spotted it, too, but I was hoping it would go away. It didn't. I call a local plumbing company, and they send someone out. I talk to the plumber as he digs deep into the ground and finds the leaking pipe.

"It's an old pipe," he assesses. "Where's the water meter?"

I don't know. Back in Massachusetts it's in the basement. There is no basement here, so I don't know where it could be.

The plumber hunts for the water meter and finds it near the rear of the property, hidden by lush tropical foliage.

I watch as he replaces the pipe and fittings so we can have hot water again. It takes about an hour for him to do the job. I feel so tired from watching him that all I want to do is crawl back into bed. It's only 11:30 a.m., and I want to hide or cry. Too much is going on. I slump into my room, sit by my bike, and put my head in my hands until my head stops hurting. Just watching someone perform an ordinary task is too much work. Before Lisa's death, I could work for days without being as tired as I am now. That was all before.

The house has some leaky faucets, and there is an armadillo or other animal digging under the house. Carl and my dad expect me to know everything about this house. I want to shout at them that I don't know. It's an old house, and this is my first time living in it. This is my first time living in another state. This is my first time as a single parent. This is my first time living without Lisa. I don't have the answers to their questions. I don't have the answers to anything. I don't even know myself anymore.

⚓

One night, after the kids fall asleep, Virginie and I sit in the living room watching Olympic ice-skating. In his room, Carl tunes in the same program. I turn the sound off on our TV set, and we can hear the show perfectly because the volume on Carl's TV is up so high. We look at each other and laugh.

How long has it been since I laughed? It feels good to share a laugh with someone.

⚓

I attend the next grief meeting at hospice. A list of words has been passed out to everyone. The columns start with the word of a feeling and then all associated feelings appear beneath it. I look at the headings: sad, depressed, happy, suicidal, and so on. I am experiencing all of the feelings, except the happy ones.

I almost start crying. I'm ashamed of my feelings. I'm irritated, annoyed, and doubtful. I'm angry with Lisa for dying.

After the meeting, I start the drive home.

"Why didn't you tell me?" I yell at Lisa.

"Why did you leave me like this with three kids? Why did you leave when I needed you the most?" I wipe at the tears as I drive.

"You could have talked to me about the fact that you were dying," I whisper, as the anger begins to dissipate. I'm angry, but most of all I miss her. She filled the biggest part of my life for the past 12 years. I miss her so much I ache from head to toe.

⚓

The boys, Virginie, Julia, and I go to Caribbean Gardens, the zoo in Naples. I feel like I am sleepwalking through the park. The sights register, but they don't interest me. Actually, I brought the kids here so they wouldn't be bored with me; I feel guilty that I've been unfocused and distant. We eat when the kids get hungry. Julia sits in her stroller and pumps her arms up and down. She's excited.

Satisfied with our expedition, we head home. After dinner, I take Julia in my arms. I haven't held her much lately because my parents give her lots of affection. It bothers me that I haven't been playing an active role in her life, and I worry that I may not have enough time to give her. Most important, I fear I may not be able to give her the emotional support and connection a daughter needs from a father. I put her to bed, and she doesn't fuss. She gives me a big smile, but all I feel is pain.

I put the boys to bed then go watch television. I hear the boys talking, and I'm grateful they have each other. I yearn to have Lisa to talk to, and I feel my spirits sink deeper and deeper. I watch the eleven o'clock news, and then I surf through the channels, not wanting to go to bed. I don't want to surrender to the darkness and loneliness. I am so tired that I eventually give in and climb into bed. I whisper to Lisa that I wish I had been able to do more for her. What else could I have done? I couldn't save her. I feel like I am drowning in a sea of guilt, and I regret the angry outrage and blame that I had directed at her.

⚓

I don't like being alone, yet I don't want to be around people. The whole two-month period of Lisa's hospital stay and death plays before my eyes. It was so strange.

I'd walk into the hospital to visit Lisa like I owned the place. Because Lisa was a nurse, I knew many of the staff who worked there. I felt like I belonged there. I would sit by her bed for hours. I'd accompany her outside for a walk or a wheelchair ride, IV pole in tow, so she could smoke a cigarette. I saw her physical capabilities deteriorating. I saw it, but couldn't and wouldn't comprehend or admit it. Now I know I was in as much denial as she was.

Tears flow down my face, and I sob so long and hard that eventually I fall asleep from sheer exhaustion.

⚓

One morning, as I drive to the company office, I find myself looking at cars in the used car lots. I already have two cars. I let Virginie drive the Volvo, and Carl drives Lisa's Olds, Big Blue. We can share the cars, so that creates no problems. But I want something that is in my name, something for me — the singular, undead person who is still trying to live.

⚓

Lisa's 39th birthday is two days away. I am starting to get nervous. January 30 was a special day when Lisa was alive. I feel itchy thinking about it. I don't know how the day is going to unfold or what I should do. I just know I am anxious because I fear I will break down and fall to pieces. Maybe I'll even die. It was the day of her birth, and now she's not here to celebrate.

We'll remember her, no matter what, I tell myself assuredly.

⚓

On her birthday, I do not die. I am calm and do not go insane. When I think of her, she will always be 38. I will always picture her at that age. Just as I can picture her on the day I met her.

Carl, my parents, the boys, and I eat lunch together at a local restaurant that serves everything from tacos to lobster. I choose this eatery because I want to order tacos on Lisa's birthday. That's what she and I devoured the night of our first date when I took her out to a little Mexican restaurant in Massachusetts.

Sure enough, Carl orders a lobster tail, his favorite, and my mind wanders back to last Father's Day. Oh, how Lisa loved to spoil her father, especially on Father's Day! For years, she would cook a huge lobster for Carl, which she dutifully cracked open for him. She never indulged herself in this feast, as scallops were the only seafood she liked.

Last Father's Day the entire house smelled like fresh lobster. Lisa called for her father to seat himself at the kitchen table. As she placed the steaming hot lobster treat before him, she blinked back tears, probably because — with Carl's advanced age — she never knew if they'd have another Father's Day together.

Theirs was a close family, brought even closer by tragedy. Lisa was the youngest of three children. Her brother Steve was six years older, and Bonda was six years older than Steve. Lisa idolized Steve, as did everyone in the family. When news reached them that Steve had been killed by shrapnel while fighting in Vietnam, they were devastated. Lisa was 12 at the time, and Bonda was already living on her own in California, so Lisa took on the role of comforter to her mom and dad.

Lisa left home to study nursing, a career to which she had always aspired, as she wanted to follow in her mother's footsteps. Lisa was out on her own, working as a nurse, when her mother died unexpectedly.

Lisa felt so sorry for her father, who was still actively grieving the death of Steve, that she moved back home to live with Carl. It was later that year that Lisa and I met.

⚓

At the restaurant in Naples, we reminisce about Lisa, which is hard for Carl and me to do. But I know we must talk about her for the boys' sake. As I munch my tacos, I tell the boys about the many Mexican restaurants Lisa and I frequented. If Lisa were here, she'd be her usual goofy self, making us all laugh. I'm struggling to keep the conversation light and lively.

Anyone eavesdropping on our conversation would think we're just a normal family enjoying lunch at a Naples tourist spot. Our upbeat conversation masks the reality of our fragile emotional state.

⚓

After supper that evening, I announce to the boys, "Here's a cake to remember Mom's birthday." It's a store-bought chocolate cake with no writing on it, but at least it's a cake. I try hard not to cry as I chew bite after bite. It could be cardboard as far as I'm concerned. I'm just going through the motions. Julia, now seven months old, is coughing in the corner, and it concerns me, so I will take her to the doctor on Monday.

"Let's go to the pet store and get some fish as a present to us," I suggest to Victor and Nick. I want to buy a present. It's what I've done for the past ten years at this time of year.

"Okay," the boys say enthusiastically.

We arrive at Pet Supermarket. Cages of hamsters, parakeets and rabbits fill the middle aisle. I head to the fish tanks at the back. I pick out a fifty-gallon tank and a stand.

"Dad, can we get hamsters?" they ask.

"I don't know." I look at the little, furry creatures. I want fish. That's why I want a fish tank. I want to see fish swim.

"We'll take care of them," they promise. "It will give us something to play with."

"Okay," I concede. "You can each pick one."

They select two hamsters. I buy the nesting material, a wheel for the hamsters to run on, a water bottle, and treats. Now we'll have a fish tank with hamsters living in it.

Victor names his hamster Peeps, and Nick names his Thunderbutt. They are active little creatures, and the kids sit and watch them as if they are watching television. They are always handling the hamsters; sometimes they're too rough with them. One day I catch them bouncing a hamster on a tennis racket. Carl threatens to get rid of the hamsters if they go near Julia. The kids are happy, though, so I'm okay with the hamsters, and I hope that they will do well as part of our family.

⚓

I delay sleep until I can no longer stand up, then I collapse into bed and fall asleep quickly. Next thing I know, Nick is climbing into bed with me. I know I should be understanding and compassionate — he's having bad dreams again — but I'm annoyed. It's uncomfortable having him in bed. He rolls over and his arms and legs flail out and strike me. His presence in the bed reminds me of what I have lost in Lisa. I sleep fitfully until around 6 a.m. I finally take Nick back to his bed. Half-asleep, I think I hear scratching in the suspended ceiling above me. Maybe bugs, I think, or squirrels. Or mice. Even rats. I turn onto my side. There is nothing I can do about it now. In the morning, I will buy rat poison.

The water in the bathtub is draining slowly. I ignore it, and it gets slower and slower. It takes me four days before I have the energy to buy a liquid drain cleaner. My misery over Lisa's death makes dealing with everyday problems overwhelming.

I am frustrated with my inability to accomplish simple tasks. I hate this life. It truly sucks.

6

A Process, Not An Event

February 1994. Two months without Lisa. At the company, I sit in Sue's office. She has been doing a stellar job of running the company for many months now. Today is my first board meeting. I find my mind wandering as business is discussed. I still think of it as Lisa's business.

As he reviews sensitive business matters related to Lisa's death, her partner, Joseph, back in Massachusetts, sighs. It is a sound made harsher by the speakerphone that delivers his voice to me. "I'm sorry I have to mention this, Rich. It's just that her death does affect the company. You understand, of course."

And I do understand. If it weren't for Lisa's partners Joseph and Philip, I would have been left without an income or health insurance. Before she died, they made sure all the proper paperwork was in order so I would inherit her share of the business. I'm grateful. But I don't tell him because it's easier to stay focused on business.

The meeting ends at noon, and I eat lunch at the office. Then I head home. I take Julia to her doctor's appointment, and sure enough, her cough is from bronchitis. She'll be on antibiotics for 10 days.

The rest of the day just disappears, and then it's 11:00 p.m. There's nothing on television that interests me, and everyone's in bed. I wander around the house, look in on the kids, study the walls, and stare into the refrigerator. I dread this time of night.

I hate it because there is no distraction from my thoughts. There is no one to relate to. My mind has quiet time to ponder Lisa's tragic death and my woeful existence. I miss her. I feel lost as to what to do. I despise this miserable life, and I want to feel better. I understand that no one can help me but me, but that doesn't make it any easier. There is nothing to do but let time heal me.

The words of the hospice grief counselor run through my brain. "Grief is a process, not an event."

⚓

I drag myself to the office. I'm numb with grief. I sit with Sue as she works because I don't want to be alone. It doesn't matter that we aren't talking; I just like having someone close. I stay until I feel a bit better, then settle into my office down the hall and read the paper. Emotions are still bubbling inside. I think of two acquaintances of Lisa's who probably don't know about her death. I begin writing them letters. As I describe the circumstances surrounding her death, tears sting my eyes. In a way, I'm glad I can weep. I'm glad I hurt. These feelings let me know I'm still alive.

I leave the office, drive around for a while, then decide to test-drive a used car that caught my eye the other day. Before driving home, I stop in at a local health spa and massage center to see if someone can give me a massage. I'm in luck; a masseur is available. I feel like a new person — at least physically — as I drive home. I should get a massage more often, I tell myself, as it makes me feel alive. Plus, it's such a welcome feeling to have someone taking care of me and my tired

⚓

muscles, even if it is only for an hour.

That evening, we all head to Red Lobster for dinner. I eat without tasting the food. Mourning or not, Victor and Nicholas practically inhale their food, and I'm once again reminded of how blessed I am to have these two treasured boys in my life. Without them, I think I would just curl up in a corner somewhere and wait to die so I could join my sweet Lisa.

⚓

Hospice night is here again. I am unmotivated and withdrawn because I know the emotions will surface tonight, and I'll be plagued by that familiar agony. These bereavement meetings are helping me, I know, but I just wish it weren't so excruciating having to work through grief.

Tonight, for the first time, I realize that many of the other bereaved spouses in the support group have it tougher than I do. At the meeting, they talk about how difficult it is to have to learn new skills, to be forced to take on a new role. Some husbands and wives admit they don't have a clue what their spouses did, whether it's homemaking tasks or balancing the checkbook.

I learn the awful truth that death can leave some folks in terrible financial shape. I listen to their anguish and feel lucky I don't have to live paycheck to paycheck, as some of these people must. Or Social Security check to Social Security check. That's even worse. I am grateful I am not in that position.

It dawns on me that, even though I have sustained a terrible loss and am deep in mourning, I am privileged. Lisa's company provided a handsome living for us. I can afford to do about anything I want. I don't have the additional burden these other grieving spouses have of needing to shrink our family's standard of living.

I also feel lucky that I don't have to learn how to be a stay-at-home dad and care for the house and kids. It's what I've been doing for the past five years.

> I think back to when Nick was about to be born. Lisa and I decided it was time for one of us to be home with the kids full time. The discussion we shared was brief and to the point; Lisa applied her logic to her family, just as she did to her business. It made more sense for me to give up my job as a technical writer than for her to leave the thriving medical device company she had founded and was managing.

At least for the moment, I feel thankful that it's comfortable and familiar being both mom and dad to the kids. I even chuckle inside as I think about what Victor and Nick have been calling me since their mom died: "MomDad." They'll start to call out "Mom," then in a split second remember she's not around anymore and add "Dad." I'm okay with being called "MomDad."

⚓

When I return home, I retreat to my room. Sure, it could be a whole lot worse, I realize, as I put myself in the shoes of the struggling widows and widowers tonight. But reality sets in, and the enormity of my loss closes in on me. It dawns on me that no matter your income, grief is grief. The searing pain of Lisa's death is totally beyond any torment I could ever have imagined.

I finally drift off to sleep. I dream I am standing in a dark, wooden building, a barn or stable, maybe. I gaze through a large opening on a sunlit woodland scene. Lisa enters. She is wearing a maroon sweatsuit. Her hips and legs are swollen like they were in the hospital. I know she wants to go somewhere, but I don't want her to leave. I hold her, and we both start crying. I want her to stay. I tell her how much I miss her.

She says she has to go, and she leaves. I accept — painfully — that she must go and I cannot stop her. I know that nothing I could say or do would stop her. Just like when she was alive.

I feel comforted by Lisa's visit with me in my dream state because it's like she was trying to reassure me of the fact that she had passed away and encourage me to begin to accept this reality.

⚓

The boys, Virginie, and I take the Naples Trolley tour. It's interesting to see some of the sights of Naples and to act like tourists in the city where we now live.

When we return home, I find a letter in the mailbox from a family friend of Lisa's. Out tumbles a picture of a grinning Lisa, the boys, and Julia. The picture was taken four months before Lisa died. It's good to see her looking so vibrant and happy. In my mind, I always see her in the hospital bed, and she isn't smiling very much.

Tomorrow I won't smile much. We are going to Marco Island to visit with the Kanes, northern neighbors of ours. They are an older couple. I know they haven't heard what has happened, and I'll have to share the sad news with them.

I feel I want everyone to know as soon as possible. Why? So I don't have to talk about it anymore. I feel like a pot of boiling water with a tight lid. I'll blow up if the lid isn't lifted, and the story isn't told.

The boys and I drive 20 miles south to Tigertail Beach on Marco Island. We enjoy the birds and the gentle waves for a while then head over to the Kanes' condo. Lisa and I met Bill and Margot Kane in Vermont ten years ago when we bought our second house just before we married.

The boys and I find the condo, are greeted by the Kanes, and settle into their living room. I tell the Kanes about Lisa. It is very hard to say the words, but somehow they tumble out.

Their faces flinch and their jaws drop. Like many people I break the news to, they don't know what to say. From my hospice meetings, I know this is not unusual. People want to be kind. They want to say something that will help and comfort us, but they don't know how.

The boys get restless. We mumble a little more meaningless conversation then leave.

⚓

On Saturday night, February 19, my old drinking buddy Chuck drives down from Tampa. He and I plan to meet up with our good friends, Sue and Joe, who work at Lisa's company. We have some time to spare before meeting them.

"Is there some place we can shoot darts or play pool?" Chuck asks.

"Yeah, Tom Fooleries. It's just up the street."

I drive. We drink some beer, play pool, and then head back to my house.

When we arrive, I'm forced to park on the street in front of a neighbor's home because cars fill my driveway. Geez, life is tough enough, I think, without having to deal with thoughtless neighbors who let their party-goers park in my driveway.

Just as I'm fuming inside, Victor and Nicholas come running over. I am still upset about the cars as I get out to see what the boys are up to.

"Hi, Dad, glad you're here," says Victor.

Nick jumps up and down. "Happy birthday, Dad!" His toothless grin looks adorable. "It's gonna be a good birthday, even without Mom here."

A good birthday? Suddenly, I make the connection.

I am walking into a surprise party for my 40th birthday. They got me!

The party features silly gifts, balloons, and a cake. I blow out the candles and cut the cake. I sit back, eating the cake, looking at everyone who is here. The only person missing is Lisa. I imagine her sitting in the swivel rocking chair, smiling, laughing, and having a good time.

Lisa liked parties. That's where we met. Our single friends used to get together monthly for a dinner party at Joe's home. My friend Carol brought Lisa to one of the parties in 1981.

When I arrived at the party, I saw Carol and this un-known woman sitting at the dining room table. I knew Carol, so I went over and sat down. She introduced me to Lisa. As Carol told me about her, I was mesmerized by Lisa's pale blue eyes. They were deep and conveyed confidence and strength. Somewhere between our lively dinner conversa-tion and dessert, a feeling came over me that Lisa was the most interesting woman I had ever met.

We had a casual dating period because I was temporarily out of work and couldn't afford to take her out often. We eventually became a couple. Two years later we married, and we had the boys within three years.

⚓

Now, after 12 years of Lisa brightening my every day, I have to do without her. And parties just aren't fun anymore.

Somehow, I find enough emotional energy to spend extra time put-ting the boys to bed. I rub each of their backs, which has become a nightly ritual, and I tell them how Mom also loved it when I rubbed and scratched her back at bedtime.

Nick's eyes well with tears. "It's your birthday, and Mom isn't here," he whimpers.

His sad face breaks my already shattered heart and soul. I pull him close. "I miss Mom so much, too," I stammer. "But on a day like today, I know Mom would want us to remember that she is just a thought away and that her love is still with us. It's everywhere. It surrounds us all the time."

Victor's voice chimes in. "I talk to Mom, just like you told me to, Dad. But I wish I could see her."

"Me too!" Nick says emphatically.

I swallow hard. "You know what? Sometimes I see her in my dreams."

Their faces brighten slightly. "Can I see Mom in my dreams to-night?" Victor asks.

"Anything is possible. We just have to stay open to Mom's love."

⚓

Days continue to pass, and I don't know where they go or what I do. One evening I ask Virginie to tend to the kids while Joe and I go for a drink at a local pub.

Joe and I arrive at the bar and each order a beer. A crowd begins to form on the dance floor, and I find it too painful to watch them. Lisa and I loved being in each other's arms and would stay on the dance floor regardless of the style of music. Rock-and-roll, slow oldies, even ballroom-style music. I turn toward the television, listen to the music, and pay no attention to where my mind wanders. If it doesn't hurt, then I am safe.

⚓

"Hey, Ritchie, it's Carol," I hear when I pick up the phone later that night. It's good to hear from her and we chat pleasantly. I'm aware of how grateful I am to have old friends. After the conversation ends, I glance at my watch. It's time for bed.

Since Lisa's death, bedtime has turned into the most depressing, restless part of my day. Before, she and I looked forward to going to bed early so we could read and have cuddle time. Now, I pace aimlessly and wonder what to do with my broken self.

I'm starting to think in terms of "before" and "now." Is it good to define the events of my life in terms of Lisa's death? Good or not, it's what I do.

I play six or seven games of solitaire on the computer. I chastise myself for wasting time doing something so useless. I disappoint myself. My rational side sees my emotional side wasting time. Yet, I continue. I just don't want to do anything or feel anything — or even think.

Sometimes at night when I am alone and resisting sleep, I have fantasies about meeting women, feeling physically close, and even having sex. Yet the thought of meeting someone is paralyzing. If I think about heading somewhere alone, where I could possibly meet women, I panic and stay home. I feel helpless and inadequate. Lisa knew I wasn't helpless or inadequate. What would she think of me now? There I go again.

Finally, at 11:20 p.m., I collapse into bed.

⚓

Lisa and I each have a car my brothers Ed and Steve helped drive down to Florida. Both cars are here; both are registered with Lisa as the owner.

On my way home from the office, I stop at the used car dealer and buy the 1988 Acura Legend that I test-drove the other day. I know I can afford to purchase a new vehicle, but a used one suits me just fine.

"Why did you get it?" my dad asks.

"I want something that is mine, in my name," I reply.

I feel empty. I need to identify with something of my own. This car is in my name. The Volvo, the Olds, and this house all have Lisa's name on them because she was the one who had the income. Everything material in Naples is hers, but she is not here to enjoy them!

Even though I made the choice to leave my job and be a stay-at-home dad, some part of me resents that I'm 40 and own nothing. Now I want something that is mine, with my name as the owner, something attached to me and not attached to her. It is a point of defiance, independence. And separation.

My dad nods. He, of all people, would understand. Ever since his stroke nine years ago, he's had to rely on my mom for everything. He can fully identify with my needs.

⚓

I arrive at the office. Sue and I chat about Lisa and whether Lisa knew what was happening to her during her last months. I get so depressed I cry. I feel on the verge of totally breaking down. I head home, wondering how often I can expect to feel so totally overwhelmed by the pangs of grief.

⚓

That evening, another friend calls. Donna learned the tragic news from Lisa's cousin. Donna is supportive and funny at the same time. Even so, talking about Lisa tonight makes me feel even more depressed. The call doesn't get close to relieving any of the misery I am experiencing. I am not yet emotionally strong enough to listen to someone else sharing good memories of Lisa when I'm in the depths of sorrow.

Home-Schooling

March 1994. Three months without Lisa. I have been home-schooling the boys for the past year and a half. They seem to like it, and I enjoy organizing lessons and guiding them through each learning activity. In my room I set up a chalkboard and school furniture. I use the chalkboard to outline lessons. The kids use it to draw pictures of video games they wish they owned.

This week, home-schooling hasn't gone very well. I've ordered a new table and kid-sized chairs, which will be delivered tomorrow. I hope the new furniture will lift my spirits and inspire me to be a more enthusiastic teacher for Victor and Nick.

⚓

It is hospice night again. While the majority of people in the group are older than I am, I agree with everything that is said because it is exactly, or close to, what I have been experiencing. Ms. Susan leads us in a discussion about denial, how painful it is to watch a loved one deteriorate because they refuse to eat, and how hard it is to say goodbye.

These discussions make me very sad, yet hospice is a place where I feel safe. I can talk about what happened and not be afraid to share my feelings.

Everyone there has been through a loss; I am not alone in my grief.

Recently, a close friend questioned whether it's healthy for me to reflect upon what happened because it makes me cry. I didn't know how to explain to him that if I can speak about it, feel sad, and cry, then at least I'm allowing myself to feel emotions. I'm not burying my feelings and refusing to deal with the enormity of being a widower at such a young age.

This is definitely crazy stuff. At least at hospice, no one treats me like I'm crazy.

I get home and sit at my desk. It's a mess. I feel like my whole life is one big mess.

⚓

After the boys and I finish their home-schooling lessons the next day, I drive to the office while Virginie stays with the kids. Spending time at the office gives me a different perspective. It's been several years since I worked in an office outside the home.

After I left my technical writing job to stay home with the boys, Lisa and I hired a babysitter to come to the house two days a week. On those days, I wrote feature articles for our local newspaper. After our helper had to quit her job with us, we hired our first nanny, Denise, which allowed me more time to write. It also enabled Lisa and me to travel to medical trade shows, where her company displayed its products at a booth in exhibit halls.

⚓

Now I have an office in a company again — Lisa's company — now my company. I bought a new computer for my office so I can write. My job at the company is to handle marketing, advertising, and trade shows. Everyone has to walk through my office to get to the lunchroom. I hate the interruptions, so I switch the lunchroom and my office. Now I have a door, and I can close it for privacy.

⚓

At times I feel as though I am caught in a vicious cycle of emotions. When I'm with my thoughts of Lisa, I want to be by myself. But physically, I want to be around people so I don't feel so alone. When I am around people, however, they expect me to talk to them, and I don't have anything to say. My feelings don't make sense to me because I've always been the kind who likes to socialize, and I used to enjoy talking to people. Everything in my life has changed, especially me.

Some of my days are a total blur. I know I have lived them, but I don't know where I was or what happened. Most days I sit in front of my computer not knowing how or what to write. I think of Lisa and what happened to her, and I weep. I am emotionally drained and exhausted. My life seems to exist only as a fragment of Lisa's life.

⚓

The boys begin their hospice bereavement classes, held during the day at Lake Park Elementary School. My sons will join other children who have lost parents. We wait in the office for the class to begin. The lobby is a long, narrow space in the front office. Ms. Susan from Hospice of Naples arrives to start the class, and the kids from the school come from their classes. Victor and Nicholas follow them while I sit and thumb through magazines.

This is the first time the boys have been in a real school while it is in session. I wonder what they think about being part of a school rather than being home-schooled. I also worry about how they will feel after the grief support meeting. Will they be willing to come again next week?

As we drive home, my fears subside. The boys are more talkative than I thought they'd be. They tell me about a fun craft Ms. Susan had them create. They made a tree of life for their family. First they used construction paper to cut out enough leaves to represent every person in their family who is still alive. They wrote the person's name on each leaf, then glued the leaves to the branches of a tree they had drawn. Then for any special person who had died, they cut out, labeled, and glued a leaf to the ground surrounding the tree.

"So Mom's still part of our family and always will be," Victor says in an upbeat voice. "She's just in a different place from us." Victor tells me about another little boy in the class who also lost his mom. Nick adds, "She died right before Christmas, too."

Obviously, they will be okay with attending more bereavement sessions. I'm relieved the class went so well, and I'm grateful to have help from hospice.

⚓

It's March, and we sit at the table facing the chalkboard. Victor is in first grade and starting to read. Nick is in kindergarten, and he's really fast in math. Julia sits off to the side in her ankle basher, the walker, and just watches. I turn from the boys to look at Julia.

Julia gazes back at me with her soft brown eyes. Her thumb is in her mouth. I study her sweet face and wonder what she's thinking. I get the feeling she's wondering why she isn't included at the big table or when it will be her turn to be the center of attention. I know I agreed to adopt Julia, and I know I love her, but sometimes I tell myself that adopting Julia isn't the right thing to do.

In fact, my thoughts have been haunted not only by the adoption, but by Julia, too. I can't put my finger on it. She's a good baby — not fussy at all. But when she smiles at me, I cringe.

⚓

In Florida, we are isolated from all my friends and family in Massachusetts. I don't want to lose touch, yet I don't always feel ready to pick up the phone and talk to people, either. So I decide to write a letter based on some of my journal entries. I'll make copies and mail them to folks up north. This way I can keep them informed about our lives.

In the first letter, I write that even though Lisa is dead, I will still be talking about her. I expect my friends to talk about her, too. They shouldn't be worried that mentioning her may cause me pain. I am already in pain, and if they choose to ignore Lisa, it will hurt me even more. It will be a denial of her life and the life she, Victor, Nicholas, and I had together.

Writing about our life without Lisa is therapeutic because it lets me express and review what I am going through.

I think I'll head back to Massachusetts in June so the boys and I can spend time with our extended family and friends in New England. I yearn to be back in our Leominster house again, the place that holds the most memories of Lisa. I'm reminded, again, of how fortunate I am that my financial situation allows me to have this flexibility.

⚓

The grapefruit tree in our backyard is still loaded with fruit, which Mom, Dad, and Carl say is sweet and juicy. I wouldn't know because I'm not a grapefruit fan, but I write to my friends and tell them if they want some to let me know. I enjoy the ritual of climbing up onto the flat roof over my bedroom to pick a new supply. Today I harvested enough to fill six plastic bags, which I place in the second refrigerator in the laundry room.

⚓

As usual, I wait until I'm fatigued to slip into bed. In the middle of a dream, I turn over in bed and bump into something or someone. There isn't supposed to be anyone in bed with me. I jump out of bed; I can hear my heart pounding. Then I realize it's only Nick. With any luck, I'll be able to carry him back to his own bed without awakening him. The little guy looks so cute in his Mickey Mouse pajamas. He stirs slightly, but doesn't wake up as I gently lower him into his bed.

⚓

I need to get out of the house, so I decide to take an adult education Italian course at Barron Collier High School. The first night of classes I arrive only to learn it's been cancelled because of low enrolment, so I wander through the building and find a ballroom dancing course.

Lisa and I had taken ballroom dancing lessons the year before, and we had a great time. Most of the people here are 10 to 20 years older than I am, but I don't care. I pay for the course by check. It is an old check with my name and Lisa's name on it.

"Where's Melissa?" the instructor questions.

"She passed away," I respond.

"Oh."

"Oh?" What is that supposed to mean? No acknowledgment of my loss? Nothing? Lisa was a delightful person, a wonderful wife and mother, and all this guy can say about her death is "Oh?" I don't know why he is ignoring the fact that she's gone. As the class begins, I realize the poor man was caught off guard and probably had no idea what to say. I let go of my anger.

As the instructor pairs us up, it's obvious there are more men than women in the class. With Lisa, I could joke easily about my terrible coordination on the dance floor. Tonight I am forced to concentrate. It's awkward dancing with a strange woman and be expected to be serious at the same time. Yet it's refreshing to be doing something in the evening other than sitting home feeling sorry for myself.

⚓

Fruit flies are buzzing all over the house. I don't know where they're coming from until I go into the laundry room, which is filled with the annoying flying critters. I open the bottom drawer of the refrigerator and discover five former grapefruit that now look like prunes. Two weeks ago, thinking the refrigerator was empty, I had shut it off.

I want someone else to clean up the stinking mess, but I know no one will. I scoop the rotten black masses into a plastic bag. The room is so narrow that I can barely open the door to remove the drawer to wash it. Ah, the joys of living in hot, humid Florida.

⚓

Julia's bronchitis was followed by tonsillitis, but both infections have cleared up now. She is her laughing, smiling self again. She can sit up by herself and is starting to creep. She lifts herself up onto her hands and knees, but then she isn't quite sure what to do next. It won't be long, experience tells me, before she is crawling here, there, and everywhere. I install childproof locks on the cabinet doors and place covers over the electrical outlets.

The adoption agency calls to inform me there has been a delay in the adoption. I'm surprised at how relieved I feel. I've been having so many doubts about whether it's right to adopt her since I'm now a single parent. I love her. I want what is best for her. Some days it seems right and other days it doesn't. When the time comes, I hope I can make the right decision.

⚓

The weather in Florida is beautiful. The balmy gulf breezes are helping to heal my body and soul.

My parents have been here for a couple of months, but now it's time for them to return home to Massachusetts. My support is leaving. It's been a great help to have my mother here to cook and give me free time. My dad has enjoyed himself in the warm weather, and knowing that makes me feel good, too.

I can't help wondering if I'll be able to fill their shoes. How can I cook when I have no appetite? How can I give to the kids when most days I have nothing to give?

I know I need to take a more active role with the kids, take charge, and all that. But it seems so overwhelming. Even the tiniest of tasks seems impossible.

⚓

Once my folks leave, I move the boys into the bedroom near Virginie. Their room shares a wall with my room, and it's across the living room from Carl. Julia is still in my room. She sleeps through the night, so she never disturbs my rest. She is such a good baby. She has a pleasant disposition and a sunny smile. I wish I could enjoy her. I like to hold her and babble to her, but my words always sound sad.

Carl is still living with us, enjoying the subtropical climate. He spends his days doing the same things here that he does in Massachusetts. He reads the newspaper, watches television, eats, and goes shopping. I thought he would want to get out more often and meet people. Somehow I forget that he's grieving too.

He has attended a meeting of the local chapter of Compassionate Friends, a grief support group for parents who have survived their children. He says he might go to one of their meetings when he gets back to Massachusetts at the end of March.

Depression

Mid-March 1994. Fourteen weeks without Lisa. The bedroom is the place my dear Lisa and I exchanged stories of our day's events, loved, and made babies together. The bed was where we shared our lives and our souls. It was the trusted comfort zone.

Now it's just a place to sleep.

I sleep well when I finally get to sleep, but getting to sleep is a challenge. The days without Lisa are painful enough, but I fear even more the stark emptiness of the night. I stay up until I'm exhausted, and then I lie down quickly. I don't want to think about the fact that I will wake up in the morning, and the nightmare will still continue. I find that curling up with Lisa's sweatshirt held to my chest helps me sleep. All I have of hers in this house is a sweatshirt and a nightgown. It's not enough.

In the morning, I don't want to get up. Why get out of bed? What is there for me? The same stuff as yesterday. Each day brings the same depressing feelings that I can't cook like I used to, or talk, or drive, or write. I know I'm depressed, and I don't care.

⚓

It's 11:00 p.m., and the house is quiet. The boys are fast asleep in their beds, and Julia slumbers peacefully in her crib here in my room. I am paying bills at my desk, which is next to my bed at the far end of the room.

Suddenly, the doors to my room slide open. At the sound, my heart jumps into my throat. I turn to the interruption and see Carl enter my room. He doesn't even look my way. He just crosses the room to where Julia is sleeping.

Why can't he knock? Why can't he give me that little bit of consideration? This is not the first time he has walked into my room without knocking. I have positioned two wicker bookcases to separate my sleeping area from the rest of the room, but it doesn't give me complete privacy. As long as Julia is in my room, Carl will continue to barge in. I finally realize I'll never have privacy with Julia here.

The next day I move Julia's crib into the small, spare room across from my room.

"Why are you moving her there?" queries Carl.

"I need my privacy." My words are quiet but emphatic.

"That poor little baby," Carl says. "She's the glue that's holding this family together."

I feel my anger rising. I want Carl to shut up. Why is he saying things like that? She's not a "poor little baby." She's not glue. She's a child living in a storm of emotions.

I'm trying to come to grips with what I feel for her, my sense of loyalty, and a nagging sense of loss, want, anger, rejection, and caring. I love Julia! I don't want to give up on her just because I'm falling to pieces.

This is not the first time Carl has assumed that we think alike. It is a thought that frightens me because we don't think alike. I'm just trying to cope with every day, cut off from my former life, family, and friends.

At least I have some privacy now.

⚓

It's time for my hospice meeting. This is weird stuff I'm going through. I've had a good week. By taking the ballroom dancing class, I have rediscovered how it feels to be alive. I have even acknowledged that women may find me attractive instead of ugly and miserable, the way I feel about myself. When I have good days, I have to take advantage of them because I know rotten days when I'm lower than my shoe will follow.

⚓

I find Gulf Shore Home-Schoolers, a group of home-schooled children and their parents. The boys and I drive 30 miles north to Fort Myers for a meeting. The only person who shows up is Jane, a single mother with three kids. We walk and talk a bit.

At the next meeting, we connect with more home-schoolers for a science class. Jane and I chat about getting together with the kids sometime. We agree that she'll come to Naples, and we'll go to the beach to watch one of the area's spectacular, renowned sunsets.

Later that week, Jane and the kids arrive at my house. The children are playing, and she and I relax in the living room. I glance over at her, and she is looking at me, but I don't know what to say. I can only think about my sorrow. I don't want to talk about that, so I say nothing. I feel like an idiot just sitting here, but I can't do anything about it. She suggests we go to the beach to see the sunset. We stroll, and the kids run. It's a lovely sunset, with streaks of fuschia and orange lighting up the horizon. We return to the house, and our visitors leave a few minutes later. I don't make any effort to get together with Jane again.

⚓

As we drive home from the boys' hospice class, they tell me Ms. Susan asked them to take turns telling the group about a favorite activity they enjoyed with their special person who died. Victor talked about sledding with his mom, who liked to go as fast as he did. Nick told the class about the songs he and Lisa would sing together and the wacky hand motions they made up for "The Wheels on the Bus." The bereaved children then shared stories about the pets they have and what TV shows they like to watch.

The three of us reminisce about Lisa, which seems easy to do today. Because Lisa was so fun-loving, we can instantly conjure up images of some of our lighthearted moments with her.

"What was Mom's favorite kind of ice cream," Victor wants to know. I grin and tell them how their mom is the one who converted me from candy bars to ice cream. "Whenever I wanted something sweet, I'd reach for a candy bar — until I met Mom," I chuckle. "Mom convinced me ice cream was much more satisfying, especially her two favorite flavors — strawberry and rocky road."

For a couple of days after the hospice meeting, Victor seems overly sensitive about things, but I don't worry about him. I know it's normal. Ms. Susan has been helping the boys work through their grief — both in the group sessions and in private counseling sessions. She also helps me understand how kids grieve and reassures me that, under the circumstances, Victor and Nick are doing fine.

⚓

The next day, I'm thankful the boys are doing okay, but I'm not sure anyone would say that about me. I head the Acura out to Interstate 75 and drive aimlessly at 90 mph. I'm trying to drive away the hurt. I'm trying to outrun the anger that is building up.

Lisa has passed away. Lisa is dead.

I hate the sound of those sentences, and the words are difficult to say.

"Why did you have to die?" I yell out. My eyes fill with tears as I pull off the interstate. "Why did you leave me with another child that I could have done without? Why did you leave me with your father?"

As I drive, my thoughts wander to Julia. I try my best to be a good father, yet I don't know if it really is my best. I ponder the thought of not going forward with the adoption. But I love her! I'm so confused.

I also think about how I dislike Massachusetts because Lisa took her last breath there. I will fill out the paperwork and become a Florida resident. It may screw up the adoption, but I don't care.

As I get closer to home, I stop yelling. I have no energy left to yell.

⚓

I sit with a therapist in her Naples office. I am here for the first of four evaluations to see if I can benefit from individual therapy. I know that I want to love again, but right now I am full of anger and bitterness. I'm depressed and overwhelmed. I will take all the help I can get.

I feel I can get through this. I'm not afraid of the work. When I was a young man, long before I met Lisa, I was in love with a woman. I knew that if our relationship ended, I would be devastated. It did end. I was devastated, and I felt like I was going crazy. But we remained friends, and I learned about love. I learned about my ability to recover from emotional hurt and to open my heart.

I will open my heart again. I just don't know when or how.

Lisa's death is the worst pain and betrayal I've ever felt.

⚓

I decide that the boys and I will go back to Massachusetts for the summer. Lisa and I had planned to spend at least six months in Florida so we could officially become Florida residents. Then we would spend the summers in Massachusetts. The legal residency consideration reminds me of the wills and trusts.

We wound up executing the final will and trust documents in the hospital because we had not finished signing them before Lisa became hospitalized. Witnesses. We needed someone to witness our signatures. I called a couple friends of my parents to come to the hospital. We stood together as I signed then handed the papers, one by one, to Lisa.

Watching Lisa's shaky hand scrawl her name on those documents — propped up in her hospital bed — is a memory I wish I could erase. Why didn't I realize she might die?

⚓

I enroll the boys in swim classes at the local community pool. Victor is making big strides. He has always enjoyed the water but never liked getting his face wet.

On one business trip a year or so back, we took the boys along. While Lisa attended the trade show, I stayed at the hotel with the kids. Every time Victor splashed water on his face in the kids' pool, he would climb out of the pool, dry his face, then go back into the water. He made a wet path from the pool to the chair.

Now he is floating and putting his face in the water without wanting to dry it.

Nick has always been at ease in the water. Now he concentrates on learning proper swim strokes and gaining more confidence. The instructors really have a handle on how to teach children. I'm pleased with how they work with the kids. It's great to see the boys taking such delight in their swimming lessons.

I sit in the bleacher seats near the other parents, mostly mothers, and watch the lessons. The boys are having a ball. I hear them giggle. I smile. It's so great to hear them laugh. Then I'm sad that Lisa is missing these magical moments. She's missing important milestones like seeing our beloved sons swim like fish.

I think back to many family times Lisa and I shared with the boys — teaching the boys to ride without training wheels as we bicycled around the neighborhood; hours enjoying the swings, slide, and monkey bars in the backyard; afternoons of sledding on the big hill down the street; taking the boys skiing for the first time.

I can see the boys like it was yesterday, decked out in their downhill ski parkas and equipment. Victor's grin was as wide as Lisa's. They were natural skiers. Nick was struggling to keep his balance, and finally his fear and frustration erupted. "Get these things off my feet," he pleaded. Nick and I enjoyed the rest of the day together, playing in the snow and drinking hot cider as Lisa and Victor skied to their hearts' content.

The clapping of proud mothers sitting in the bleachers below brings me back to the present. Lisa's not here to witness the boys' swimming accomplishments; she'll never share a milestone again. The familiar waves of widowerhood envelop me, and I hide behind my sunglasses.

Then out of the corner of my eye I spot Victor and Nick waving to me from the deep end of the pool. I wave back and give them two thumbs up. I'm so proud of both of them!

Gut-Wrenching Decision

End of March 1994. Four months without Lisa. "Add these numbers," I say to Victor. We are at the chalkboard in my schoolroom/ bedroom. He's not paying attention. Nick is running around, and Julia is sitting in her walker behind us.

It's getting to be too much. They don't want to learn, and I'm frustrated with them. I turn and look at Julia. She sucks her thumb and stares at me. She seems to be saying, "What about me?" I quickly turn back to the boys because I have no answer for her. Before she gets much older, I'll need to provide that answer.

I know the early childhood years are very important in forming bonds with parents, and I want Julia to have a strong foundation in life. But I fear that I cannot give her the emotional support she needs. And if I can't, then I have to figure out who can, and time is of the essence.

I turn to the boys. "If you don't pay attention, I'll send you to school," I threaten. I'm drained. I have to lie down.

Two days later as I am reading the *Naples Daily News,* I see an ad for an open house at Seacrest Country Day School. I call and make an appointment.

⚓

Yesterday, Victor was complaining about an itchy spot. I looked and saw one red bump, but I didn't think much of it. Today, his body is covered with them. I take him to the doctor and learn he has the chicken pox. It won't be long before Nick and Julia get them, too.

⚓

It's nighttime, and I am watching Julia sleep. What a little angel she is! I can provide for her financially, and I feel strongly that I love her. I believe I can be a good father to her. When Lisa and I were meeting with adoption agencies, they knew that if Lisa's illness progressed, I would be able to take care of a child. I agreed to adopt Julia to make Lisa happy. Although I love babies and enjoy caring for them, it doesn't mean, as a single parent, that I wanted more kids. I didn't believe Lisa would die, and I thought we'd parent Julia together. Parenting by myself changes things, and something just doesn't feel right.

I go back to my room and stop at the chalkboard. I turn and look where Julia was sitting earlier today and remember how her eyes were questioning me. What would it be like for her to grow up with a father like me? She would have the material things, and she would know that I love her. But is that enough? I know something is missing.

She would feel a distance between us. I don't want Julia growing up feeling something is wrong with her when there isn't anything wrong with her. I'm the problem, not Julia. I'm emotionally closed. I can't give to her or even to myself.

I hope she can forgive me, and I hope I can forgive myself, but I decide not to adopt her.

I've tried to make this work. For three-and-half months I've searched for the feelings, and I haven't found them. Julia deserves to be cherished, respected, and loved, and she will be. But not by me. I can't do it. Finally, I know that for sure.

The next morning, I call the adoption agency.

"I'm not going to adopt Julia," I inform Jennifer, the counselor.

"We were wondering how you were doing," Jennifer admits.

"Can you find another family for her?"

"Yes, we'll call you back."

I've done it. I'm committed. I'm scared.

A few days later the agency calls back. They have a family. Now they want to know how soon I can return Julia to the Massachusetts adoption agency. I plan for the beginning of April, around Easter, which is just around the corner.

The process seems so fast. I expected it to take longer. It seems I don't know the meaning of time anymore. I'm scared and shocked but a bit relieved it will happen fast.

I tell Virginie.

She agrees. "I think it's best, too."

I call my mom and dad and they are sad, but they understand. I tell my brothers and sister, who also validate my heart-wrenching decision.

"I'm giving Julia to another family," I tell the boys.

"But she's our sister," they both cry out.

"She needs more than I can give." They still don't seem to understand. Then an idea pops into my head.

"But now you could marry her because she isn't your sister," I point out.

Their mood is a little brighter.

Now I have to tell Carl. This is not going to be easy. He thinks Julia is the one holding us all together. Maybe she is the one keeping *him* together. She's the future to him. She's a replacement for the girl he lost. Lisa was death and abandonment for him, and Julia is life.

I invite him to join me at the kitchen table for a glass of juice. We settle into our chairs, and I blurt out, "I've made a tough decision, Carl. "I'm not going to adopt Julia."

"What?" his face displays alarm.

"I can't give her the emotional tie she needs. She deserves better. The adoption agency has found another family for her."

His face twists, and tears well in his tired eyes. He can't fathom how I can give up this beautiful baby. He can't comprehend why I'm tearing this family apart. I'm doing it because it is the right thing to do for Julia.

I write to my friends back home and inform them of my decision. I also tell them that if they plan to try to change my mind, they don't need to bother. This has been the most agonizing decision I have ever made. If they were in my shoes, they would know what I have gone through to reach this torturous point.

I make plans for Julia, the boys and me to arrive in Boston on the first of April. The boys and I will return to Florida — without Julia — a few days after we talk with the adoption agency officials and meet Julia's new family.

I phone my attorney and ask him to draw up a trust fund for Julia. I may not be able to support her emotionally, but I will make sure this little girl is provided with some financial support. I feel Lisa would approve.

⚓

The days are warming and the nights are cool. It's great sleeping weather when I can get to sleep. I still dread the night. The house is quiet and dark. I'm alone with my thoughts, which are running rampant. I'm struggling with feelings of guilt about giving up Julia. It seems one minute I'm at peace with my decision, then doubt and fear cloud my head and my heart, and I'm not sure what's right anymore. This is the time when I need Lisa the most, but she's not here. We were a good fit when it came to making decisions about the kids. I yearn to have her beside me.

⚓

Carl returns to Massachusetts at the end of March. It was good to have him here, but frustrating, too. The loud TV; the fact that in the kitchen, he would inevitably stand in front of the counter I needed to use; his constant intrusions into my room. I couldn't blame him. He was just being himself. When we lived up north, we built him an apartment in our huge house so he wouldn't feel he was in our way. And he could turn the television as loud as he wanted. There, we had ample room for everyone. But here in Florida, the space has been far too cramped.

While I get frustrated having Carl around, I feel a special kinship. Lisa was so good to her father, a devoted daddy's girl. I know his sorrow is deeper than anyone can imagine.

I hope and pray that Bonda will make an effort to stay in touch with him. I know their family has been through several tragic deaths, but Bonda and Lisa had been so close, especially after their brother Steve died. The sisters' closeness tightened when their mother became terminally ill; they would talk by phone weekly, if not daily. After their mother died, the girls made a point of including Carl in their vacation plans. In fact, when Victor and Nick were toddlers, we all traveled to Sweden to visit their Scandinavian relatives. Our entourage included Bonda and her teenage sons, as well as Lisa and Bonda's cousin Cheryl.

⚓

Days pass in a haze, and I find myself waiting for the plane to take us north. Before I know it, we are parking the car in the lot near the adoption agency in Massachusetts.

I balance 10-month-old Julia on my right hip. The boys are walking on my left as we cross the street to the adoption agency. I feel eerily calm as we enter the building. Victor and Nicholas play with toys in the hallway while Julia and I are led into Jennifer's counseling office. Jennifer and I take turns babbling cute phrases to Julia. We're waiting for the new adoptive parents to arrive. Jennifer tells me they have an adopted son who is two weeks older than Julia, so they're quite excited about bringing Julia into their family, too.

The new parents join us and we chat easily about Julia while she plays on the floor. We discuss her schedule, her food likes and dislikes, her delightful disposition, and the fact that she will probably be getting the chicken pox. Then I leave the office so Julia's new mom and dad can spend time with her alone.

In the hall, I am surprised to see the birth mother and grandmother, even though I'm well aware this is an open adoption. The birth parents meet the adoptive parents, so Julia will know her heritage. We exchange an awkward hello. I don't know what else to say to them. The last time I saw them was three months ago when I told them Lisa had died.

I am called back into the office. We discuss details and agree that tomorrow I will return with Julia and leave without her.

⚓

The house is somber. Carl is not only broken up about losing his daughter; he is now losing a granddaughter. He can't comprehend why I must give Julia up. He can't grasp what I'm going through. I can't understand what he is going through, either. My saving grace is that he doesn't try to change my mind.

Later as I tuck Victor and Nick into their beds, I hum the first line of the Beatles' lullaby, testing myself to see if I can sing it to the boys without breaking down into a sobbing mess of a father. Victor comes to my aid by singing the lyrics, followed by Nick. We sing a bittersweet rendition of the entire song, then give each other extra goodnight hugs and kisses.

⚓

"It's going to be all right," I keep repeating to Julia as I carry her into the adoption agency. "They are good people with a good home. You'll have a mother, father, and a brother your own age." I want her to know it will be all right. I want to reassure myself that it will be all right.

In Jennifer's office, I talk with the new parents and Nancy from the agency. Julia sits on the floor playing with the doll the new parents brought. I don't have much to say. The mom picks up Julia and coos at her in a loving, playful way. Then the dad takes her in his arms and plants a kiss on her rosy cheek. Obviously, they are thrilled to have another child, especially one as special as Julia.

The time has come for me to leave.

"See you later," I say to Julia. "Everything is going to be fine." Her big brown eyes lock onto mine, and I recognize the questions she's projecting: Where are you going? Will you be back? Why are these strangers holding me?

I can't look at her anymore. I leave the office. Nancy walks me to the door. She is speaking, but I don't know what she is saying.

"Are you going to be all right on the drive home?" Nancy asks.

I look at her. "Yeah," I lie, "I'll be fine." I don't move toward the door.

"Would you like a hug?"

"Yes."

I hug her and start sobbing. I didn't think my heart could break anymore, but it has. I've given a child away, and I feel like a piece of crap. I had a choice, and I made it. "I know it's right," I keep repeating to myself, but it doesn't make me feel better. I wasn't her birth parent, but I was her parent. God, please forgive me for what I've done.

I stop crying, leave the building, and get in my car. I am drained physically, emotionally, and spiritually.

I also feel relieved.

I visit with friends in Massachusetts. They tell me I did the right thing and that they are not sure they would have had the courage and wisdom to make the same decision. Courage, wisdom? All I know is that giving Julia away feels almost as gut-wrenching as burying my lovely Lisa.

⚓

The boys and I return to Florida. Carl stays in Massachusetts. I think about Julia all the time. One day I get a call from Julia's parents. Julia has come down with the chicken pox. We talk about our visiting them. I agree that our first visit with Julia will come next year, giving them a year to settle in as a family. I look at the calendar and realize that I have given Julia away on the day before Easter.

I was raised in the Catholic Church. Easter is the time of new life. Julia is starting her new life, and I can't help but be amazed at the timing. This synchronicity brings me comfort.

Openings

Mid-April 1994. Eighteen weeks without Lisa. The boys and I arrive at Seacrest Country Day School, the one I read about in the newspaper, and visit the classrooms in session. I am amazed at the small class sizes. The first grade is working in small groups, and it reminds me of home-schooling.

Each classroom boasts a teacher and an assistant. I can feel the care and concern the teachers have for the students and see the respect the students give the teachers in return.

In the office, I flip through the volunteer notebook where parents sign in when they help at the school. Some parents are able to give only a few hours while others fill pages with volunteer hours. I like the fact that the school encourages parents to participate in their kid's classes. This means I can still be part of the boys' education.

I am very impressed with the school. I feel the boys will get the extra attention I want them to have since their mother is gone. They'll be able to work at their own pace in the class. For the first time since Lisa died, I'm able to make a decision quickly: Victor and Nick will attend Seacrest.

I arrange to have them grade-evaluated next week. On the way home, they ask if we can stop to buy school lunch boxes and other supplies. They are brimming with excitement about going to a real school.

I love teaching them at home, but I've lost my motivation. And when I'm depressed, frustrated, and impatient, I'm not bringing out the best in them. In a year, if they don't like Seacrest, I'll go back to home-schooling. If they like the school, then we'll live in Florida 10 months of the year and visit Massachusetts according to their school schedule. It will mean our summers in Massachusetts will be shorter, but we are all ready for a change. I desperately need a change.

⚓

The other night I went to visit Sue and Joe. We were watching television when the song "Hero" by Mariah Carey came on. After Lisa died, Sue's daughter, Erica, had written out the words to this song and given them to me because, to her, Lisa was a hero. When the song came on at Sue and Joe's, tears started coursing down my face. There was no sobbing, just tears. After I plopped into bed that night, the tears kept flowing.

⚓

I'm better today. I learned at hospice that what I had is called a "grief attack," an acute upsurge of grief that can occur without warning. It can come out of the blue. Anything can set me off. I feel like I'm walking through an emotional mine field.

I'm supposed to live life as I did before, but I can't. When Lisa died, parts of me died, too. Everything is different now. It feels like I'm going crazy.

I pull out the bookmark hospice gave me that lists what one might expect during intense mourning. I've read these words a hundred times, but it helps me stay sane to see them in print once again: "You might feel like you're going crazy." I know that this feeling is normal. Not easy, but normal.

⚓

A new friend who is a real estate agent phones me to say there's a condo for sale in a prime location in Naples, which would make a great investment property. We meet at Park Shore Resort, where I tour three available units. I decide to make an offer on a single-bedroom unit that has a good view of the pool and restaurant. The offer is accepted, and I buy the condo. Buying property was a project Lisa and I used to tackle together. This is the first piece of property I have ever bought alone.

⚓

Lisa and I had been dating for several months when the subject of real estate came up.

"I'd like to buy a house with no money down, fix it up, and sell it to make money," she said one night within our group of single friends.

My father had always told me stories of houses he could have bought that are now selling for ten times the amount. I was broke, and I didn't want to remain broke, so Lisa's idea and my dad's idea made me agree with her. The only other person interested was our friend, Tony. The three of us started looking at property from Vermont to the north shore of Massachusetts.

After six months of searching, Tony dropped out due to his work schedule. Lisa and I spent another three months looking from Cape Cod to Vermont. Every house or duplex we considered buying just didn't feel right, or it needed too much work. Then we found a three-room cottage in Southeast Massachusetts.

I walked in and saw the kitchen/dining/living room area. It had open stud walls. I thought it was the perfect project. The other two rooms were bedrooms. A well and septic system provided the home's water and sewage disposal. We talked about it and decided it was the ideal house to renovate and sell later for a profit. Real estate books said it could be done, so we bought it with a very small down payment and secured an interest-only mortgage.

We chose to listen to the people who said we could make money that way and ignore the advice of nay-sayers. It was a big risk, but when we were together, Lisa and I felt like we could tackle anything.

Every weekend for the next year we worked on the house. With plenty of energy and laughter, we installed insulation, sheetrocked walls, hung wallpaper, painted, and enjoyed our getaway. At night we played the "what if" game, such as what if you had a child and a certain situation came up. It was a testing process for each of us. A year later, we sold the house — nearly doubling our investment — and went out to buy our second investment property.

⚓

Now I have purchased my first property without Lisa, and I still own the second property we ever bought together. Will this be enough to help me regain a better sense of self-worth? I can only hope so.

I have begun meeting people outside the small group of friends I already know. The depressing part is the thought of dating again. It was hard enough when I was in my twenties. I wasn't very self-assured. It will be harder now that I'm 40 with two kids. I have to start somewhere. It's going to be strange enough for me to see myself with other women; I also have to get other people used to seeing me with someone who isn't Lisa.

⚓

Nicholas did catch the chicken pox from Victor, and he is finally over them. The poor kid had them everywhere, even on his eyelids.

Both boys are getting brown from their trips to the beach with Virginie. It is heartwarming to see how happy the boys are. Each time they come home from the beach, they head to the backyard where Virginie stands with the hose, spraying salt and sand off the boys while they giggle themselves silly. I'm so lucky to have a nanny, and so are the boys. This way, they get to do fun things with someone positive like Virginie, rather than being stuck with their grumpy, depressed dad all the time.

⚓

As I drag myself through the house, I realize how sick I am of the dingy brown color scheme in this place. The shag carpet is light brown. The wallpaper is a faded yellow brown. A section of the living room wall is covered from floor to ceiling with smoked mirrors. Part of the arched wall that divides the living room from the dining room is covered with tan wallpaper with black markings. I lift up a corner of the wallpaper and take a peek to see what is underneath. It's just a plain vanilla wall. I tear the paper off all the dining room and living room walls. It's an improvement, but now it needs paint.

I paint the living and dining rooms white, which makes a huge difference. The house — and my outlook — seem brighter. I pull up a corner of the carpet and discover tan terrazzo floors that are cooler on the feet. I cut the carpet into pieces and throw it out.

Progress.

⚓

Seacrest School calls to tell me the results of the boys' evaluation.

Victor is ready for first grade, and Nicholas is all set for kindergarten. The school confirms what I already know: Nicholas is good with numbers, and Victor has good auditory and visual memorization skills.

I was worried about the evaluations because if their scores were bad, it would mean that I wasn't a very good home-school teacher. I only finished half a year of first grade with Victor and half a year of kindergarten with Nick. The fact that they tested well means I did well. What a relief! I had been beating myself up about being an ineffective home-school teacher, and now I learn that I can actually pat myself on the back for a job well done!

The boys and I frequently talk excitedly about their going to Seacrest in September. While this is the end of a chapter in our lives and I'll miss teaching them at home, I know I'll be around to educate them about other lessons in life.

Phases

Late April 1994. Twenty weeks without Lisa. The boys and I wait at the Fort Myers airport for my mother and father to arrive. They are going to help Virginie with the kids while I travel to a trade show in Nashville for Lisa's company — my company, now. We shift from foot to foot, waiting for passengers to come out of the gate area.

"Is this the flight from Boston getting off?" I ask a young woman standing near us.

"I hope it is," she says.

I feel a tug on my sleeve. It's Nick. I bend down to hear him.

"Is she going to be our new mom?" he asks.

"No, Nick, I just asked her a question." I hold his hand. My heart breaks. He's only five, and it's clear to me he wants his life back, too.

⚓

I see myself going through phases. I don't like the one I'm in now because I'm angry at Lisa for leaving me and abandoning our precious young sons. This is the cruelest irony of bereavement: the person I depended upon to help me in the tough times is not here in the most challenging moments of my life. Anger bubbles up often, then I get angry with myself for being angry with Lisa. It wasn't her fault. How heartless I am to blame her!

⚓

Thank goodness it's hospice night again. As luck would have it, Ms. Susan brings up the topic of anger. "No feeling is a bad feeling," she stresses. "It's what you choose to do with the feeling that matters." Then we take turns talking about how each of us vents our powerful emotions in healthy ways.

I leave the meeting feeling relieved. At least I haven't chosen to vent my anger by doing destructive things to myself or others. It could be worse, and I need to remember that the glass isn't always just half empty when one is widowed. It's also half full.

⚓

Phil and I are in Nashville to exhibit Lisa's invention at a nursing show. This is the first show we've attended without Lisa, and I'm amazed I can still talk about Cath-Secure to nurses who stop by our booth and that I can do so without getting choked up and teary-eyed.

During a slow period, I decide to take a break and stretch my legs by walking around the huge exhibit hall. The rows upon rows of medical equipment take me back to Lisa's hospital stay. The machines she used, the pumps, the color of the room, her declining health, and the talks we didn't have. Assaulted by memories, I quickly retreat to the safety of our own booth. At the end of the day, I head back to my room for a nap.

I meet Phil later for dinner. After dinner, I don't feel up to leaving the hotel for a night out on the town, so we each head back to our own rooms. I watch TV to pass the hours.

The next day I venture from the booth to find something to eat. I sit by myself at an eight-seat table. Six nurses ask if they can join me. Space is limited, and I don't mind. I tune into tidbits of their conversation and hear that the nurse sitting across from me recently lost her husband. My heart aches for her, and I mention that I am also newly widowed. The woman to my left turns to me with sympathetic eyes. We chitchat for several minutes. Her eyes and her genuine concern pull me in. Later in the show, I seek her out. Why? Why do I want to be near her?

I want to feel connected. I want the feeling of aliveness again, of love, and of being special in someone's life. Talking with her gave me that feeling, and I want that again. I want more of it, but I learn that she is engaged and lives on the West Coast.

The next day, Phil and I return to Florida.

⚓

Sex.

It's something I haven't had and haven't missed. I'm thinking of it now because I have a spontaneous erection. It's the first erection I've had in months. It's amazing to know that this part of my body still functions.

I have been reading the personal ads in the newspaper. I'm searching for someone. I need to connect. I need the relationship and the feelings I had with Lisa. I call the numbers listed in some of the ads, listen, and hang up without leaving a message. I answer one from a young woman. She calls back and wants to meet me. I am flattered that a young woman is interested in meeting me, and we make arrangements to get together.

She calls me the day we are to meet and tells me to bring $250. She wants money? This is just a sex thing? How stupid I am to think someone would just want me for me! I'm angry that I was taken in by the ad.

But I go anyway.

I sit on the sofa in her apartment and she shows me some pictures of her in a bikini she wore for the Miss Hawaiian Tropic beauty contest. Ooops! In the middle of the stack are a couple pictures of her in the nude. She wonders how they got there. I know. This is just a setup, but I accept it for what it is. We talk, and before long, she has removed her clothes. I also undress, and we proceed into her bedroom.

My physical urge is fulfilled, but the emotional closeness that I seek is not. I drive home on automatic pilot. A mile from the house I start to cry. I sob because I have been unfaithful to Lisa. I know I can't cheat on a dead person, but it doesn't matter. My emotions know what happened. I've been unfaithful. I've been stupid. I've been desperate.

⚓

A few evenings later, Virginie and I sit on the couch talking. I want to touch her, but I don't. She works for me, and taking care of the kids is her job. I can't break that trust. Yet, I just want to feel normal — the way I did with Lisa. I want to be held. Virginie is close, but I can't cross that boundary. We just talk.

⚓

My dad's sister, Aunt Jo, has arrived to spend a week with my parents before they leave to go back north. Virginie's parents and sister have come from France to Florida, so Virginie is taking two weeks off. They'll all stay with us. I think this diversion from routine may be good for all of us.

I recall other diversions. Lisa could be impulsive. One time, a few years after we were married, she called me from the office on a Monday and asked if I would like to go to Bermuda.

"Some day, sure."

"Good. We're leaving Saturday."

And we did — with two toddlers and Lisa's father, Grandpa Carl. A good time was had by all.

Then I remember the boat. She loved motorboats and insisted we purchase one after we were married. I reluctantly agreed. She named the 16-foot yellow outboard "Honeybee."

The first day she took Honeybee out onto the lake, she ran aground, ruining the propeller. I promptly bought a new one. Lisa crouched next to me as I took off the broken propeller and replaced it. All the while, she shared stories of boating mishaps with me, including the times she ran out of gas while boating with her girlfriends in New Hampshire. I glanced up at her to see if she looked as pleased with herself as she sounded. Yep. That was Lisa — always ready for fun and adventure!

⚓

I find that eating ice cream is easier than dating. With ice cream, I can pick out the flavor and the toppings. It's exactly what I want. I don't have to talk. There is no emotional involvement.

I don't know what to say to women. I realize that I'm needy, very needy. I want them to care for me, to give to me, to touch me, to fondle me, and then to leave me alone. I can't give to them because I have nothing to give. I've had my life uprooted and scrambled, and I need input to make me better. I have nothing to give.

Sally is an attractive widow close to my age who comes to the grief support group. She is easy to talk to because we share the same experience of losing a spouse and having young children. We get together for dinner with the kids at a restaurant or at her house where the kids play, and she and I talk. This is a stepping-stone in learning to communicate with a woman who isn't Lisa.

Sometimes, when the kids aren't there, we massage each other's shoulders and backs. It leads to sexual touching, yet we don't have intercourse, and I don't touch her below the waist. She tries to kiss me, but I turn away because kissing is too intimate for me. I'm afraid if I tell her not to kiss me, she will reject me and not want to see me, and I need the attention.

I want sex, and I need sex, but I am so mixed up. I'll take all the touching a woman will give me, but I will give nothing back. Part of me understands that this attitude is self-defeating and needs to change. Someday.

Sally lends me grief books to read. A quote by author Stephanie Ericsson captures the essence of where I am in my grief process: "How do you piece together something that may someday resemble a life again? Not without many hours, days, months, even years. Not without blisters, cuts, bruises, and tears. And the only place to begin is in the shadow of the mountain."

⚓

The tears, I find, are totally unpredictable. I'm embarrassed to cry, and when I do, I cover my face when people are around. The problem is I never know when I'll start to sob.

I can't listen to the radio in the car. The love songs cause grief attacks, especially songs by Lisa's favorite artists like Neil Diamond, Elton John, and Aerosmith. If I tune into talk shows, I find their subject matter has no relevance to my life today. I drive in silence, and I like the silence, even with my negative thoughts.

A song can make me cry. A sign can make me cry. A thought can make me cry. It seems almost anything that reminds me of Lisa and her love will make me cry. I know I weep for what I have lost. I wonder if some of the tears are from fear that I may never find love again, or even tears of fear that I might.

It doesn't matter where I am or who is around when an attack of grief comes upon me. I just have to roll with it. I have to let the tears come and wash the grief from my soul so I can live again. The words of Ms. Susan from hospice have become my mantra: "It's okay to cry. Tears help let the pain out."

Some days I feel there is no reason to live, and then I see the boys. They are my reason.

⚓

Victor, Nick, and I drive to Orlando for a few days of normal fun at the theme parks. During the four-hour car trip, we listen to cassette tapes of children's songs. I can almost hear Lisa's melodious voice joining ours and picture her playing her guitar and singing, "The wheels on the bus go round and round, round and round, round and round. The wheels on the bus go round and round, all through the town." I glance in the rearview mirror, and sure enough, Nick's hands are moving up, down, and everywhere as he acts out the hand motions he and Lisa made up for this song.

At Universal Studios, we check out the Ghostbusters attraction and ride the Earthquake. The next day we meet up with longtime friends, Chuck and Trish, and visit SeaWorld. We take lots of pictures as we wander through the Arctic Exhibit. Then the boys want to sit in the splash zone for the Shamu the Whale show. Trish and Chuck decide not to sit with us in order to stay dry. Smart choice.

I shake my head and playfully warn the boys, "We're going to get wet."

"We want to get wet," the boys assure me.

During most of the show, only a few drops of water come our way. Then whoosh! The show ends with a huge wall of water sweeping directly at us. The boys are in shock. They don't look too happy about being drenched to the bone. They also plead with me not to take a picture of them, but I ignore their requests and squelch a laugh as I click the camera. It's an experience that feels goofy and normal. Oooo-kay!

On Monday, Trish joins us at EPCOT. Tuesday, the boys and I return to Universal for more rides. I'm going on the rides, too, because the boys are so enthusiastic about them. It would be all the same to me if I just skipped the rides. What a party-pooper! If it weren't for the kids, I would have stayed home. But I can't refuse them fun in their life just because I can't enjoy my own. Thank God for these two terrific kids!

⚓

My brother Ed is flying south to see us, and at the end of his visit, he will drive Lisa's leased car, Big Blue, back north. I am grateful my brothers have helped me with the cars because I wouldn't have survived the long trip with two energetic sons in the back seat.

I wish I had the ability to enjoy life like the kids, but my grief is full in my face, and it's hard to see around it. Kids grieve differently from adults, according to Ms. Susan. They take grief a little at a time, then play as kids do, then grieve a little more. I noticed how true this was when each hamster died, and we held a little burial ceremony in the backyard. Minutes after the burial, the boys were ready to play.

Sometimes the boys are disagreeable, and I have to remember it is their way of grieving. When they have questions about their mom, I answer them and emphasize she will always be a part of us. She will always be in our hearts. As they get older, they will understand more and want different information.

"Dad," asks Nick, "are you going to get married again?"

"Yes," I reply.

"What if our new mom doesn't like us?"

"Then I won't marry her," I reassure him. "We're a package. She has to take all of us. If she doesn't want all of us, then I won't marry her."

It's as simple as that.

Memories

May 1994. Five months without Lisa. Mother's Day is approaching, and I am nervous and sad at the same time. I anticipate it will be a hard day. I know I can handle it, but it hurts when I think about the kids.

> Last Mother's Day, Lisa was out of the hospital and feeling pretty chipper. Victor and Nick created a giant heart-shaped card for her and made some funny-looking gifts from Lisa's craft supplies. Using pipe cleaners and pine cones, they crafted a zany-looking family, which was supposed to look like each of us. Lisa howled with delight at the silly faces the boys had painted on the pine cones.

⚓

This Mother's Day I can't think clearly, but I decide to take the boys to the service at Unity Church. Afterwards, we stop and buy half-a-dozen roses. "We're going down to the pier," I tell the boys.

"Why?" they both want to know.

"I thought it would be nice to remember Mom on Mother's Day by throwing some flowers into the water. You know how much she loved roses, especially pretty pink ones like these."

Nick frowns. "What was the name of those yellow flowers Mom liked? Daffy-something?"

"Daffodils," Victor answers. "But Dad's right. Mom liked pink roses best."

I park the car and give each boy two roses. I take the other two and we stroll along the Naples pier. Since it's 85 degrees and sunny, I feel conspicuous in long pants and dress shoes. The boys are wearing shorts. It seems everyone around us is in a bathing suit. We reach the end of the pier and gaze into the blue-green water.

"Here's to Lisa. I wish you were here." I toss my flowers into the water. The boys throw theirs in, too.

"Happy Mother's Day, Mom. I love you," Victor says softly. "Me too," echoes Nick. "And I hope you like the pretty flowers," he adds with a grin.

While Victor inherited Lisa's strong jaw and big blue eyes, Nicholas inherited her fun-loving nature, spontaneous personality, and determination.

⚓

Phil and I attend a trade show in San Antonio. I bring Virginie and the boys with me so we can fly to Massachusetts afterward for the summer. While I work during the day, Virginie takes the kids around town. When I have time off, I take the boys sightseeing because it is my first time in San Antonio, too, and it gives Virginie time off for herself.

The boys and I enjoy a boat ride along the waterway, a bus tour of the city, and a visit to the Alamo. We poke around in a western museum, and I take a picture of Nick on a fake horse out on the sidewalk. They are such good travelers and a sheer pleasure to be with. When the show ends, we fly straight to Massachusetts instead of Florida.

For the first few days back, I wander aimlessly around the big house. Besides Virginie, the boys and myself, there is Carl, Carl's niece Cheryl, and her husband Don. Even with its 10 rooms and Carl's apartment, the house seems crowded. We let Cheryl and Don use the bathroom to get ready for work before the rest of us get up. That helps a bit, but we still feel the crush of too many people.

The only person missing is Lisa.

I feel her loss so much stronger here than in Florida because we lived here, made love and babies here, headquartered the business here, and we had parties here. Now, even with all the people residing here, this house seems superficial and empty.

⚓

I try to occupy myself with business matters. In a conversation with my accountant and a lawyer, the subject of where Lisa lived and died comes up. There are state taxes to pay, and it makes a difference in which state she died. If she died in Florida, we can avoid some taxes. While she actually was in Massachusetts when she died, if I prove we were intending to move to Florida, it's possible to avoid the tax. My lawyer is doubtful I could prove a case; my accountant says I should give it a try. He sends me home to gather proof.

I climb into the attic and sit in front of boxes of receipts from the previous five years. All of our activity has been recorded in dollars and cents. I start to pile up credit card receipts, travel expenses, and all the little bits of paper that I've kept from our life. It is slow going at first because each slip of paper triggers a memory of our life together.

When I finish, I realize why I felt our life was rushed; we were always on the go. The figures show that in 1989 we spent 28 days out of state, 48 days in 1990, 60 days in 1991, 100 days in 1992, and in 1993, Lisa's final year and in spite of her illness, 193 days.

To further my case that she was a Florida resident, I pull out papers showing that we bought a house in Florida, that we filed a letter of intent with the Collier County Public School System in Naples to home-school the kids, and received a confirmation of acceptance to begin home-schooling.

I submit the tax information and wait. Eventually, the Massachusetts Department of Revenue rules that Lisa was a Florida resident, and I don't have to pay a Massachusetts tax. I make a note to myself that with my quarterly tax payment next month, I want to make a donation to hospice.

⚓

As I roam around the house, I feel the absence of Lisa's spirit and laughter. Her clothes and all the physical accompaniments of her life are where she left them, waiting for her return. Her body and spirit will never be back to claim the clothes, books, and collectibles that defined her, and each one has a memory for me.

I never realized how I defined who she was. I know how she looked, now I am surrounded by the clothes she wore, the books she read, the makeup, the colors of the rooms, the placement of souvenirs, the mementos of her late mother and brother. Each item embodies another aspect of the woman I loved, and each object reminds me she is no longer with me.

In our upstairs bedroom I open the two closet doors, one hinged left and one hinged right. They swing out into the room to display the clothes and the full-length mirrors on the inside of each door. My dress shirts, suits, and shoes are on the left. Lisa's dresses, blouses, skirts, and slacks hang on the right.

I look at her clothing, and each article brings back a memory of when I saw her wearing it. I touch the mauve sleeveless silk dress she wore on our last wedding anniversary. We spent the weekend in Boston, dining at an upscale Mexican restaurant and treating ourselves to a play.

As I glance at the garments, it's obvious that rosy pinks and various shades of red were Lisa's favorite colors. She not only looked great in those hues, she used them to decorate the house. The carpeting in every room downstairs is decidedly dusty rose, and the kitchen wallpaper is cream with tiny mauve-painted flowers.

The knowledge that she will never wear this slinky dress again — or any of these clothes — is sobering. I know that I have to give them away, but I can't part with anything of hers right now. It has been only five months.

I reach my arms around the clothes and hug them, enveloping myself in the scent that still, even faintly, lingers in each fiber.

If I get rid of her belongings, I would be getting rid of her, and I can't do that. I can't part with the memories of our life. I've heard of widows getting rid of their mate's wardrobes right away, cleaning out the memories as soon as they can. For me, that action doesn't feel right. It feels like I would be trashing her memory.

Yet I believe I must start removing the signs of her life. I must move on and return to the person I was before, yet treasure the experience of being married to Lisa.

I see several pocketbooks on the floor and decide to start with these because they are small, and I never really paid attention to them when she was alive. What can they hold that would affect my life?

I sit cross-legged on the carpet and grab a medium-sized black bag, snap it open and find spare change, matchbooks, scraps of paper and the cellophane tops from packs of cigarettes. I remember seeing her dropping the coins into her purse after making a purchase. I toss the coins into a jar. I take each piece of paper, read it, and decide whether it's a memory I want to keep, or if I just need to toss it out. Then there are the cellophane tops of cigarette packs.

> How many times over the past ten years did I see her open a pack of cigarettes, crumple the cellophane and tuck it into her pocketbook? I can't recall. It was a ritual no matter where we were: skiing, riding in the car, or just coming out of the store. She was a light smoker, maybe two packs a week. She was smoking on the first night I met her, and I can still recall the cigarette held between the fingers of her right hand, the look on her face, her eyes, and the shape of her mouth when she inhaled and exhaled the smoke.

I finger the cellophane, and a slight hint of tobacco hits my nose. When did she put this one in the purse? Was I with her or not? What year was it? I can't recall, yet I know that this was part of her, a repetitive habit that I saw numerous times and can easily recall.

I lay down the first pocketbook, open a dark blue bag, then a small black bag. The contents are similar to the first: coins, paper, cellophane and memories.

I snap open the fourth pocketbook and stop.

Each piece of paper, stray note, or trinket doesn't just remind me of Lisa, it brings her to life again. I know she is dead, and I don't want her to be dead. I want her to be alive.

I can't continue with the purses.

I lie back on the bedroom's forest green carpet, and an emotional storm unleashes its fury from my heart and mind. My cheeks are drenched, and my chest aches. I want Lisa to help me with this loneliness and pain. I want her to help me cope with this yearning for what will never be. I want her to put her arms around me and tell me that everything will be all right. I want, I need, but I don't receive.

I close the closet doors to the memories. I sob.

⚓

I find a young widow and widowers support group in town, which meets at the Pilgrim Church. This is the same church where we were married, the boys were baptized, and we held Lisa's funeral. I haven't been in the church since the funeral.

"Which side of the bed do you sleep on?" asks Mary, the facilitator.

I picture our bedroom. I am now sleeping on the side where Lisa used to sleep.

"If you sleep on your mate's side, you could be afraid of seeing that empty spot in the bed."

Lisa and I used to change sides of the bed every now and then, but now I occupy the side that was most often hers. When I go to bed that night, I move onto my side. I look to her side. I reach out my arms as if to hold her and find it's an empty space. Mary was right. I don't like seeing that space empty.

I sleep on my side of the bed but eventually drift back to the side that was hers. I know I'm there, and I accept that. In Florida, I don't have that problem because Lisa slept in that bed only one week, so there is no side that was hers. It's just my bed, and I'm the only one in it.

⚓

The boys want to visit Kay, the counselor at Emerson Hospital where Lisa died. I'm glad they like spending time with Kay. I know they enjoy taking turns talking to her and playing video games in her office.

Walking into Emerson Hospital is very strange this time. It has been almost six months since Lisa died. On the fourth floor, the hallways intersect in a 'T' formation. To my right is Four North — Lisa's floor, the floor where she died. In front of us is the pediatric wing, where the boys are going, and to the left is Wheeler 4, were Lisa used to work.

A flood of memories assaults me. The New Year's Eve that Lisa was hospitalized, I dressed in a tux to spend the evening at her bedside. Her close friend Gail, who worked at the hospital, came down from her floor to ring in the New Year with us.

The photographs lining the hospital walls conjure up images of the watercolor I bought because it reminded me of our group of close friends. Our group. Lisa's and mine.

I recall the countless hours when Lisa rested in her hospital bed, eyes closed, listening to my voice. Fondly, I think of the ski trips, especially the one on which I proposed. It was at Mt. Snow, Vermont, the day after Thanksgiving — first day of ski season. I couldn't wait till we got to the top, so I popped the big question while we rode the chairlift. Before we reached the summit, her pastel blue eyes sparkled with happiness. She said "yes," and changed my life forever.

I drop the boys off with Kay, and I turn toward Four North. I take a deep breath and go through the double doors.

The business of caring for the ill or dying is taking place as usual. I had walked down these halls a hundred times, yet this trip seems the hardest. A couple of nurses recognize me and ask how the boys and I are doing.

"Fine," I reply. "Just visiting. The boys are on the next wing visiting Kay."

I survive my trip on the floor. I return to the 'T' intersection of the wings to sit and read the newspaper. Familiar faces walk by. Some say hello; others just pass by without noticing me.

I'm beginning to feel ill-at-ease in this building.

⚓

It seems like I have moved sideways. I see my life as being lived in a parallel universe. It's so familiar, yet not quite the way it was. I have a closet full of women's clothes but no wife to wear them. I'm living in Florida when I wanted to stay in Massachusetts. I have two sons, and I used to have a daughter. I have a nanny who takes care of the kids and also helps to keep me from falling, yet I know I should be taking charge more.

Each day is the first day of its kind. The first visit to Four North at Emerson Hospital.

All those firsts. The first day without her, the first month, my first birthday, first wedding anniversary, first Valentine's Day, first Mother's Day, July Fourth, vacation day, and so on. There are 365 first days of life without Lisa, and the boys and I have been through only half of them.

I have to say goodbye to every first day. There are hundreds of other farewells I have to say. Goodbye to going to the store with her; to puttering around the house with her; to watching a movie with her; to savoring precious moments with our sons.

The biggest goodbye is to the life I had before. The little ones include the hundreds of places or things we used to enjoy together. If I experience them alone, and survive, then I can say goodbye and put them to rest.

I don't know where it will end, if it ever does.

Where am I emotionally? I am not sure of what direction to go. I have not settled down to an emotional base point where I can say, "I have arrived." Arrived where? I need to find the place where I am comfortable to be the "me" I was before Lisa died. I don't know how far back I have to go.

I find myself wanting to seek out old friends, trying not so much to reestablish the friendship, but to see if the connection with them feels right. How far will I have to go? I don't know. I only know that I need to find out. I need to stop the descent of my emotions and steady my grip on life.

I feel like a teenager — so young, with a world of possibilities. I can be anyone, and I can have anything. Yet, unlike a teenager, I have kids who need nurturing, and I have money. I can have any material object I desire, but I can't buy back time. I would give up the money if I could get Lisa back.

Money is no comfort for the loss of a loved one. I discovered that truth when I received her death benefit check. Insurance companies urge everyone to have life insurance on our loved ones. Yes, the money is important to pay off mortgages and bills. It makes the daily struggle for survival so much easier. I am extremely fortunate and know it.

I have been poor and in love, and I have been rich and in love. I would give up all my material possessions if I could have the love of my life back by my side.

Living Again

June 1994. Six months without Lisa. It has been six months since Lisa died, and I still wear my wedding ring. I am not a married person any longer, yet I don't see myself as single either. The ring says I'm married, and I know I need to take it off at some point, but it is a big step.

I spin the ring around my finger. I slide it off and slide it back on. I take it off and can see a faint tan line. My finger feels cold and exposed, not quite right. I put the ring back on. I take it off again and place it on the nightstand beside my bed. I feel naked without it. I look at the ring on the nightstand and it seems out of place. It should be on my finger. Picking it up, I read the inscription inside — TMHLL3/1/86 — which means, "To my husband, Love Lisa" and our wedding date. Her wedding ring bears a similar inscription.

We used to sign cards with our name and then a string of initials like LAL, which is Love Always Lisa, or YATB, which is You Are The Best. The fun part was to see if she or I could decipher what the initials meant. Sometimes we could do it without help, and sometimes we would need the other as an interpreter. Anyway, my ring is now on the nightstand, and her wedding ring and engagement ring, attached by a safety pin, sit in our safe deposit box.

The swath of exposed skin feels cold relative to the rest of my finger. It is a heightened sense of awareness because the ring has been on my finger for eight years. Besides a watch, it is the only piece of jewelry I wear. I feel naked and unfaithful, yet I leave the ring off for the night.

The next morning I slide the ring back on. I'm not ready to show the world I am single. I will tell the world I am single, and I will tell them I am widowed. But right now, I still need the security of the ring because, though single, I still feel loyal to Lisa.

When I meet new people, it's important for me to tell them I am a widower. I don't want them to think I'm divorced. I imagine if they believe I am single, and that I have custody of the kids, then they'll think my "divorced" wife must have been an awful person. Lisa was anything but that, and I don't want people to think for a second that she was a bad mother. She was a devoted mother to the boys and an incredible wife and friend to me. So I'll tell people I'm a widower and admit to myself, again and again, that I have lost my wife.

She was more than a wife. She was my best friend. What started out as an attraction — those amazing eyes just pulled me in! — grew into a mating of souls.

It didn't take me long to comprehend that Lisa was a woman who had ideas and acted upon them. Through her years of nursing, she was determined to find a better way to secure a catheter on a patient's leg. The existing products used at the hospital where she worked — if anything other than plain tape — were awkward, inconvenient, or down-right painful. Lisa had the courage not only to invent her own product, which she called "Cath-Secure," but also to start her own company to produce and market it. Other nurses at trade shows I attended told me they thought about inventing a similar product. But Lisa was different — she acted upon her ideas.

Like most people, I had ideas, too, but didn't act on most of them. Lisa and I bought real estate together, went canoeing, took ski trips together and dreamed together. After a year of light dating we became a steady couple. Our friends were surprised when we announced we were getting married. I was 32, Lisa was 31, and it was the first marriage for both of us. Now, eight years, four houses, and two kids later, I'm a widower.

There wasn't enough time in our relationship. We needed more time together. A day longer, or an hour, or a minute longer would have made my life richer, but then I wouldn't have been satisfied, and I would still have yearned for more. I wanted 40 or 50 years with her, this intelligent woman with the hypnotic eyes — this soulmate who showed me how to love and be loved.

Two weeks later I take the ring off again. I tape it to a piece of paper and lay it on the nightstand. I tape it so I won't lose it. After surviving three days without wearing the ring, I realize I will never wear it again. It now sits next to Lisa's wedding ring in the safe deposit box, where it will stay until I decide what to do with these treasures from our eight years of marriage.

⚓

My friend Donna calls. We met years ago when I was doing a feature article on local artists. She is traveling to Italy for a month of studying, and she invites me to travel around Italy with her for the last week of her trip. I would like to go, but I don't want to leave the kids. I don't want them to worry I might abandon them.

I want to go, but I don't want to betray Lisa's memory. Donna and I had always been just friends. But what would it be like staying with her for a week? I don't know what she's thinking. Would our relationship remain platonic?

Getting away might be good for me, though. I am torn.

Eight years ago was the last time I was in Italy. With Lisa. On our honeymoon. Can I go back there and be with a different woman? Can I visit sites Lisa and I enjoyed years before? Can I be me and travel by myself? I question all of it: me, Donna, Lisa, and what it all means to my life and Lisa's memory.

What about the boys? Can I leave them and just take off for a week? Don't I need to be home with them? Don't they need me with them? Can I be without them? Can they be well without me?

Donna leaves for Italy without knowing my answer. A week later I decide to go. I contact her and we agree to meet in Florence during her last week of study. Then we'll go to Rome.

I call my parents, who agree to watch the boys while I travel. I arrange my flights, stuff necessities into a small backpack, and depart.

I fly from Boston to Zurich, Switzerland, where I make a connecting flight to Lugano, Switzerland. During the three-hour wait for the final leg of my trip, I buy a bottle of water at the café and take it outside to sit in the shade under the umbrella at one of the patio tables. Behind me the stone houses seem to sit on each other as the hill rises. The small airport lies in front of me, the mountains rising beyond the airfield.

A mixture of Italian, French, and German languages floats through the air. I am calm just sitting and being quiet, yet, at the same time, impatient to get going. Finally my flight is ready, and I depart for Florence in a small turboprop plane. The flight is brief, and, on approach, the plane banks over hills of red-tiled roofs.

Donna and her Italian friend meet me at the Florence airport and drive me through the town to the small hotel where Donna is staying. I drop off my stuff and we set out into town.

Donna is very animated about the beauty of Florence. She leads me down short, narrow streets to the Ponte Vecchio. She describes it as if she were reading from a travel book. "The Ponte Vecchio is the bridge of goldsmith merchants that crosses the Arno River. It was built in 1345 and again in 1564, when stone arches were added."

We saunter into and out of stores cantilevered over the sides of the bridge. It is crowded with people walking from one side of the river to the other. In the evening, we eat at an outdoor café in a small piazza; later we stroll to the Pitti Palace Art Museum for a classical music show in the inner courtyard.

The music is classical harpsichord, and during the intermission we get drinks.

"Do you like it?" asks Donna.

"It's okay," I reply.

"Do you want to leave?"

"Yes."

She smiles as we walk away.

⚓

We wander the streets then return to her room on the third floor in the pensione, or guesthouse. It's midnight, the windows are open, and the air is humid and stagnant. We become intimate, but all I can think about is the boys. I start to panic.

I told the kids I would call, and I haven't called yet! I am so far removed from home and from my life with Lisa. I feel the tears running down my cheeks. I must call the kids.

Donna says I should wait until morning, but I can't. I must do it now. I have to try. I need to know that I have tried.

They are my world, and I need to be in touch with my world. The need is overpowering. I feel possessed.

There's no phone in the room. I get dressed, wipe the tears from my eyes and leave the room. I mutter to myself: I told them I would call. If I don't call them they will think I am dead. I can't let my kids think I'm dead. They need me, and I need them.

I fly down the three flights of stairs and out into the humid night. Crossing the cobblestone street, I enter a large hotel. I tell the desk clerk I need to use the phone. He directs me to the booths. I go into one and try to call home. I can't get through. I try my charge card and dial. Nothing. I try again and get nowhere. Damn Italian phones! Why can't I make a straight call to the U.S.?

I am dejected and frustrated, but I don't feel like I am going to crack. I've tried, but I couldn't get through. That's okay.

I still feel alone as I trudge up the stairs, collapse into bed, and fall asleep.

⚓

In the morning, I help Donna pack her art supplies and pictures so they can be taken back to the States without damage. She needs shipping tubes for the pictures, so we find a hardware store. Donna explains her needs to the clerk, and I add a few words of Italian to help. The man from the hardware store understands and walks us over to the art store. He asks if I am Italian. His compliment makes me realize my fluency in Italian is better than it was eight years ago. Well, maybe all I spoke on my honeymoon was the language of love.

We buy the tubes, finish packing, and carry all our stuff to the train station.

We take the train to Rome and find a room nearby at the Hotel

D'Este. Donna talks the desk clerk into taking her to the beach the next day.

While she goes to the beach, I will visit my relatives. They are my mother's cousins; Lisa and I met them on our honeymoon. I call them so they know I am coming. I take the subway to the bus depot, then board the bus for the half-hour ride to Artena. I must go there to tell the family that Lisa has died.

I sit with Ezio and Adella in their kitchen. Ezio is my grandmother's nephew. They speak no English, yet we communicate easily, and I tell them Lisa has passed away from cancer. They tell me about their son who drowned. We sit in silence with our losses.

I go next door and visit with Ezio's brother, Silvio. When it approaches time to catch the bus back to Rome, Silvio drives me into town to the bus station. I arrive back in Rome tired but happy that I have made it to my relatives' house and back. Some victories are small ones but, nevertheless, welcome.

I am thankful that I have survived a memory. I have been some place that Lisa and I had been together, and I have been there alone. It is closure for me, and I know I am all right with it. There is more grief work to do in this city.

Donna reports she had a good time at the beach and entertains me with her adventurous story of getting there. Tomorrow she is leaving. I help her pack a carry-on bag and cushion the onyx eggs she bought as presents. I agree to take this bag with me because she has so many bags and paintings to take back.

I accompany Donna to DaVinci airport, we load a cart with her bags, and she gets in line. Army personnel in the airport, carrying Uzi machine guns, watch the crowd.

The airline agent talks to Donna. They ask me to stand back, so I oblige. Donna and the airline representative talk alone. Donna comes back and tells me they were asking who I was and if I had given her anything to carry on board. It is my first experience with the fear and caution of terrorism. Donna departs through the gate and is gone.

⚓

I have three days alone in Rome before I return to Massachusetts. As I walk from the Piazza Navona, the Spanish Steps, and on to Trevi Fountain and Piazza Republica where Lisa and I had visited, I try to feel her presence. But I don't sense her presence in any of these places. The people have changed, and I have changed. I am here as a single person.

I survive my visit to each site that held memories of Lisa. I make peace with each museum, fountain, or antiquity, and claim it as a part of my past with Lisa and part of the present that includes just me. It is a small step, but an important one. It fills a hole in part of me. After three days of filling holes, it is time to leave.

I fly out of Rome to Zurich to change planes for Boston, and I place my bag and the one I am carrying for Donna on the scanners. Her bag beeps.

"Did you pack this bag?" asks the female attendant.

"Yes." It's true; I did pack it.

"Will you open the bag?"

"Yes."

I don't know what they are looking for, but I open the bag. The attendant starts to look for something. She pulls out a woman's folded nightgown, high heels and silk scarves.

This must look strange; a single man is carrying a bag with women's clothing in it. Wrapped in the scarves are the onyx eggs that Donna bought as presents, which had set off the alarm. The attendant is satisfied there is nothing dangerous and I am cleared to go. I repack the bag and walk away. I start to grin as I walk, imagining what they must have thought of me with women's clothes.

I arrive back in Boston. I exit from customs and see my mom and the boys. I hug them all. God, it feels so good to hug them!

I didn't realize how much of life I was not living until I returned. I am calmer with the kids, I feel more confident, and I'm glad I made the trip.

I just hope this renewed lease on life will last.

Goodbye to 'Firsts'

July 1994. Seven months without Lisa. Nothing is inevitable except death, taxes, and junk mail.

I receive mountains of mail with Lisa's name on it, yet I'm not ready to stop her mail. I would be telling the world she is dead and I am a widower. If it is company mail, I keep it, and if it is for both of us, I read it. If it is true junk mail, I throw it out. I hope if she never answers, the senders of junk mail will eventually stop.

⚓

Victor's birthday is a big day, and that means Lisa should be here. I think Victor will be fine today, even though it's his first birthday without his mom. I'm not so sure about myself, though. I'm feeling weepy and hope I don't spoil the fun by breaking down in front of everyone.

Victor is turning seven years old. I'm amazed at how big and mature he has become. It's hard to believe that seven years have passed since Lisa and I were speeding down Route 2 to Emerson Hospital for his birth.

I remember as if it were yesterday. Minutes before getting into the car, between contractions, Lisa had been calmly organizing her desk so the business she operated would run smoothly while she was in the hospital. She always thought of how to make things easier for someone else.

Words seem inadequate to describe the utter joy we felt when we first held our precious little boy. That day was the first of many magical days we shared as doting parents.

We were a terrific team when it came to raising the boys. I feel so inadequate as a single parent, especially on special occasions like today. I've sent out the invitations and ordered the cake. It's a Batman cake. We add our own special decoration to the store's cake, just as Lisa used to do. I'm a little anxious as the guests arrive, but I don't give in to my feelings. I hold onto the cordial smile and festive mood. The kids run around the yard before and after we devour the cake. It's good to have my friends around. Their support has been a lifesaver.

⚓

After the party when everyone leaves and the kids go to bed, I am alone. I find that the days leading up to "special days" are the hardest. I worry that on the special day I will break down or crack up. It's funny to think of those emotions as a direction. On the special day itself, I am less anxious or nervous than on the days preceding it.

For Victor, today was his first birthday without his mother. For me, it was the first birthday party I've thrown for him without Lisa's help. We're all taking important steps toward healing.

⚓

It's time to think about the future because Virginie's year in the States will be over in November. Virginie doesn't cook, but she's a godsend when I need time for myself. She is also someone I can talk to, which is a big help to me. We discuss American life and how it differs from her homeland in France. The conversations force me to think and concentrate. As we battle through these days, weeks, and months without Lisa, Virginie keeps our family on an even keel. It's hard to imagine someone else filling her shoes.

But I figure I will need to arrange for another nanny.

⚓

The boys, Virginie, and I go north to vacation on Balch Lake in New Hampshire. Our family has vacationed here many times over the years. The initial days generate some emotional bumps because it is the first time the boys and I have been here without Lisa.

The house we're staying in has three bedrooms. Virginie has the room near the living room. The boys' room and mine are off the kitchen on the other side of the small ranch house.

At night I am in my room in bed holding one of Lisa's sweaters to my chest, as I've done for months. I can't bring myself to get close to other women, but I still need something from Lisa to be close to. Her turtleneck sweater brings me comfort.

During the night I hear a loud thud. I run to the boys' room and find a sleepy-eyed Victor climbing back into the top bunk.

"Are you all right?" I ask.

"Yeah."

The next morning Victor is quiet and holding his right arm.

"I'm going to take him to the doctor," I tell Virginie.

We learn that Victor has broken his arm and has to have a cast. Luckily, it's a fiberglass cast he can get wet, except we are warned he shouldn't swim in lakes because dirt or leaves could get underneath the fiberglass. How frustrating! It's the first day of our vacation on a lake, but Victor takes these limitations in stride and fishes instead of swims.

⚓

Virginie takes the kids on canoe rides and swims with Nick. To give her some time off, the boys and I visit a neighbor's house where they can play with two girls about their age. The kids play while we adults drink beer and chat about the kids and our houses.

For the Fourth of July, we drive to Wolfboro on Lake Winnipesauke to watch the fireworks. The traffic is so snarled that it takes us two hours to get out of the small town, giving me lots of time to reflect upon the many fireworks displays enjoyed with Lisa.

"You would have loved tonight's show," I silently whisper to her.

The next night, I decide to show the boys how to build a campfire. A fire pit stands in the front yard of the vacation home. There is no lawn; it's just sand and stones located over the leach field of the septic system. I'm pleased that Victor and Nick are adept at lighting the fire. Then we bring out the marshmallows and teach Virginie how to toast them. In France, they eat marshmallows uncooked. She likes the cooked ones. This is another food she will bring back to France, along with peanut butter and Jell-O.

Our nights around the campfire bring back memories of when I used to light campfires as a kid growing up in New England. Good memories, untinged by the sadness of life without Lisa.

⚓

Another highlight of our vacation is a visit from our good friend, Allan. He was Lisa's friend in high school, and when Lisa and I were dating, she introduced me to him. We hit it off instantly and have been close buddies ever since. He is still single but says he is in "like" with someone. I hope he'll someday find the right person.

⚓

Back in Leominster, I lie on the couch in the living room, mentally listing all the "firsts" without Lisa. Paradoxically, each first is emotionally draining yet strengthening at the same time. I have survived so many firsts, and I have survived saying goodbye. I have said farewell to the fear of meeting people for the first time without Lisa and to the fear of doing things for the first time without her. I guess this is progress in my journey through grief.

The summer is flying by. I'm still getting letters from the lawyers as they settle Lisa's estate and move everything into my name. Lisa is now being referred to as "The Estate of Melissa Johnson Ballo."

⚓

I visit Lisa's gravesite for the third time since we arrived back in Massachusetts. I know that only her body is here and that her soul is in the spirit world. Yet I find it easy to talk to her here. This is the resting spot for her physical remains, the place where I last saw her body. I view the headstone, staring at the comforting etching of the lighthouse. Then my fingers trace the letters of the name "Ballo." As I touch the headstone, I tell her how much I love her and miss her. It still seems so strange to see my last name on a gravestone. It seems even more surreal to read the back of the grave marker: "Melissa Johnson, Jan. 30, 1955 - Dec. 14, 1993, Never give up."

My Jewish friends have told me about a gravestone ceremony — called an "unveiling" — usually held within a year after someone dies. I like the idea and decide to hold the ceremony this summer rather than waiting until December, when it will be too cold for an outdoor gathering.

Thirty friends join me for the unveiling of Lisa's grave marker and for a sharing of fond memories. I tell the story of a ski day when Lisa tromped into the lodge and threw her wet gloves on the table, knocking over a friend's beer. Others share their stories. We laugh and, through shared memories, bring her back to life for a short time. It feels great to be able to remember her and the good times we had without crying or feeling depressed. Afterward, everyone congregates at my house for pizza and beer. This is the first time since Lisa's death I'm with my northern friends in a social situation that isn't a funeral. Another first for my list.

⚓

The summer is almost over, and the boys are back at Emerson Hospital talking to Kay as I sit in the lobby and read the paper. Kay takes me aside and tells me the boys are coping fine. She suggests a professional therapist to help the kids, if necessary, and informs me they don't need to come back to the hospital for counseling sessions.

I am taken aback. Not return to Emerson Hospital? The boys were born here. Then on and off for more than three years, Lisa was a patient here, since the first operation to remove the malignant tumor, to her dying days last December. I have been here with Lisa through each surgery, chemotherapy session, and other tests and medical procedures.

The boys have been visiting Kay for the last year. This hospital has been a destination, a place of refuge, a source of sorrow and of comfort. And now Kay wants us to stop coming? How can I? How can I separate from a place that embodies both life and death for me?

⚓

A week has gone by, and all I can think about is the separation from Emerson Hospital. I come to terms with this necessity on my path toward a new life: my reasons for going there are gone. Lisa's not there, no one else in my family is ill, and we are coping well without counseling. It's time to say goodbye to the hospital. It doesn't mean we can never stop in and say hello; it just means that visits there will no longer be part of our routine.

I talk it over with the boys, explaining to them what I've come to accept. They can visit with Kay and everyone, but not as a regular part of our lives. It is time to move on. Both nod their heads. They understand.

We make a final visit to the hospital so the boys can see Kay. I stop by the nurses' station on Four North to say goodbye to the nurses there.

"I hope my husband does what you did," a teary-eyed nurse says as she gives me a hug.

What did I do that was so different? I was doing what was normal for me — loving my wife and being there for her no matter what. I can't understand why a husband wouldn't be there for his wife.

Maybe my situation was different, I think. Some men might not be able to leave work for days, weeks or months during a wife's illness. Maybe that's what the nurse meant — that she'd hope her husband would put her as his top priority, regardless of what that might do to his career.

As I turn from the nurse's station, I say farewell to Lisa's old room. I say goodbye to the walls, the floors, and the sounds of the hospital. I walk through the doors that close it off from the rest of the hospital. When the boys are finished, we drive away and I say goodbye to Emerson. Another part of my life is put to rest.

⚓

In the auditorium of St. Bernard's Catholic School in Fitchburg, we find our seats at the front. A few months ago, Lisa's business partner, Joseph, asked if I wanted to donate money to have the library named for Lisa. This was the school his children attended, and knowing how much Lisa believed in the importance of teaching kids to read, Joseph thought naming the library for Lisa would be meaningful to me.

I agreed, and tonight is the awards night and dedication of the library. I feel awkward being here. The boys and I receive a plaque similar to the one that will be hung in the library. Because I want something tangible to speak of Lisa's life, I hope the kids using the library will read the plaque. They didn't have the chance to know her, but through this gift they'll feel the impact of her generous heart.

⚓

I say goodbye to my friends as the boys, Virginie, and I get ready to fly south to Florida. There is not much to pack. I have one final thing to do — return Lisa's leased Oldsmobile to the dealership. It seems strange to be driving Big Blue for the last time, and I grin thinking about Lisa's unusual taste in cars — they had to be big with tons of chrome. As I pull Big Blue into the dealer's lot, another chapter comes to an end.

On August 30, my mom and dad drive us to the airport. We all exchange lots of hugs and kisses as we say goodbye. For what must be the hundredth time in recent months, I realize how much I love my parents — how crucial they are in my life.

On the airplane, I sit between the boys. They're elated, because the feature film is *The Mighty Ducks 2*. Nicholas sits on my right armrest and Victor plunks down on my left armrest so they can see the movie better. I am squished between them. I want them to move, but I let them stay. My mild annoyance is swept away by the warm sense of family closeness. It doesn't get much better than this!

Thoughts turn to Lisa and the undeniable reality that she is not here to share this family moment. My grief work has prepared me for this sense of loss, of future hopes and dreams that will never be fulfilled. The pain is not quite as sharp as it was a few weeks ago.

⚓

As I age, in my mind Lisa will always be 38 and beautiful. The sorrow is intense, but I can handle it better now, which means I don't cry as often, especially in public. Being able to acknowledge the pain and work through it is new for me. I can sense that my self-confidence is building, step by step, day by day. I feel like part of me that died is coming back.

⚓

The flight from Boston is not direct and we have to switch planes in Atlanta. We are standing in line to check in for the next leg of the trip. More accurately, I am standing in line as the boys run around like heathens and play with the stanchions. I know Victor and Nick are bored. They are only five and seven and don't like to wait.

I feel frustrated and inadequate. The kids are driving me crazy, and when I tell them to stop, they ignore me. I grab their hands, and they just squirm away. I don't want to lose my place in line. I sigh. I wish Lisa were here to help, and then I get angry with her for not being here. I want to run away and disappear.

Just when I thought I was taking a step forward in my grief process, this "inadequate parenting" stuff feels like two steps back.

I turn to look at the line of people behind us. An older man says to his wife in a voice loud enough for everyone to hear, "It's easier if there are two parents."

I'm dumbstruck. Did he really say what I heard? Should I let him know why only one parent is present, make him regret his quick — and inaccurate — analysis of the situation?

I can't think of a comeback. I don't know what to say in return or how to say it. I turn back to the counter and check in, avoiding eye contact with the rude man.

We board the plane, and again, I am sandwiched between the boys and feel alone. I think about what the man in line said. I should have replied something like, "My wife would love to help, but she's dead," or, "My wife would gladly help, but she passed away." I rehearse different possibilities, but the chance to say them has long passed.

What he said was true — it *is* easier for two parents to corral two rambunctious young boys. He didn't know why their mom wasn't with us. Can't blame him for speaking the truth.

I forgive him. I wish I could forgive myself — and Lisa — as easily as I can forgive a complete stranger.

New Chapter

September 1994. Ten months without Lisa. Virginie, the boys and I arrive back in Naples. The boys are excited to be starting their first year of school. Virginie's year with us concludes at the end of October, and she'll leave for France in November. This is a troubling thought because she has helped me so much, both with the kids and personally. She helps me daily in small ways — often just by being another person in the room when I feel alone.

⚓

Naples is hot and humid. To avoid the miserable heat of midday, I take walks early in the morning. I am getting used to the heat, or at least how to deal with it. I fill a "solar shower" bag full of water, let it sit in the backyard sun all day so the water is hot enough for an outdoor shower. As I fill the shower bag, I feel a rush of air by my head and hear a thump on the ground. A green mass the size of a football lies at my feet. I look up into the tree above me and discover it's an avocado tree. I've never seen avocados grow before, and now they're trying to hit me. Life in the subtropics is never boring, that's for sure!

⚓

The hot water pipe breaks again, but this time the damage is located under the driveway. To repair it, plumbers have to crack the concrete and dig a ten-foot trench diagonally across the driveway. It's an old pipe, they remind me.

⚓

The boys, Virginie, and I head over to Seacrest Country Day School for a "meet your teacher" morning the day before school starts.

We enter Victor's first grade class where he meets his teacher, Mrs. Linwood. She hands Victor a list of things to find in the classroom such as his desk, his name on the birthday board, and a bottle of Elmer's glue labeled with his name. At the art island, he is invited to draw a picture. Mrs. Linwood then introduces Victor to four boys who will also be in his class. The boys all say hello to Victor, but Victor seems to have lost his voice. He can't return their greeting. This is one of the few times I've seen him speechless.

Next, we head over to Nick's room to meet his teacher. As Nick hides behind me, I introduce myself to the teacher. He finally peeks out, meets Mrs. Smith, and sets out to find the items on his list.

When it's time to go, I can't get the boys to leave. They want to talk to Mrs. Smith and show her how high they can count.

Thursday morning, the first day of school, they are so anxious that they bounce out of bed at 6:00 a.m. Class doesn't start until 8:30, so we have lots of time to enjoy a leisurely breakfast. Just before we pile into the car, I grab my camera and take a snapshot of them. Getting them both to smile is impossible — Victor can't stop grinning, and Nick looks miserable.

I walk them to their classrooms. Victor gives me a quick goodbye kiss, but Nick doesn't want to let go of my hand. I give him an extra hug and tell him I'll see him at 2:30 when I pick him up. I'm not sure who it's harder on — Nick or me — to have to say goodbye.

That afternoon on the way home, the boys chatter gleefully about all the things they liked about school, their classmates, and what they're looking forward to doing in class tomorrow. Nick is as enthusiastic as Victor, and I breathe a huge sigh of relief.

Each morning they are up and ready for school without prodding. I'm glad they like Seacrest so much. They are making friends, and they seem to appreciate having a fixed daily schedule. While they're at school each day, I go to my office at the company. Handling the marketing doesn't take much time, so I work on my freelance writing. Writer's block overwhelms me most days, so I don't get much done. But at least I have some place to go, which is better than sitting around the house feeling lost and lonely.

Ray, a longtime family friend, and I decide to join a gym as a way for us to get in shape and socialize. While Virginie stays with the kids, I meet Ray at 6:00 a.m. at BodyQuest and work out for a couple of hours. What the experts say about exercise is true — it not only makes me feel better physically, it also lifts my spirits.

⚓

All things considered, the first month of school has gone well. Victor is eager and ready to go every morning. He likes the kids in his class and enjoys getting there early so he can hang out with his friends.

Nick likes school but seems reluctant the last few days. He says he is having a problem with being teased, and he doesn't want to go to school. This morning the teacher had to pry his fingers off the door to get him into the classroom. It isn't easy for me to walk away and leave him looking so sad and desperate. Thankfully, the teacher called me mid-morning to report that Nick was doing just fine.

That evening, my brother Ed calls and talks with Nick about school.

"Have you made any friends yet?" Ed probes.

"Yes," Nick blurts out, "and she's getting on my nerves."

Nick is always straightforward with what he thinks.

This new chapter in our lives is difficult for me. I find it challenging to have to separate from the boys. They are moving into a new environment, and I am still in my old one. They are making new friends, and I remain rather isolated. While I am meeting other parents at the school through my volunteer work, making new friends isn't easy for me.

Even though our days of home-schooling are over, I'm thankful I can still participate in the kids' education. Today is the kindergarten field trip to the Collier County Aquatic Center, and I am a volunteer driver. Nick and two of his classmates ride to the pool in my Acura. I enjoy hanging out at the pool where I can get acquainted with other parents. When I realize I am the only father there, I imagine the moms think I am divorced or just a dad helping out with the kids. It's hard for me to admit I am a widower; such an admission would let the pain in.

I've dealt with this same feeling too many times to count, but it still isn't easy. I remind myself that everyone's grieving process is different. Maybe saying the word "widower" wouldn't faze some men. For me, the word carries a power I can't deny. It's an issue I'll continue to work through.

⚓

I've decided to see a therapist because I have so much work to do on myself. I meet with the doctor to tell her about my life and why I think I need to see her. The words flow effortlessly as I open myself to her. She agrees that one-on-one counseling will be helpful, and we schedule an appointment.

⚓

Today after school, we visit the pediatrician. Nick has developed a cough, and Victor has a paronchia, an infected blister on his left index finger, which he got by jamming his finger while playing soccer at school. They are both put on antibiotics.

Two weeks later we return to the pediatrician's office. Victor's finger is fine. He is a fast healer; his broken arm was mended and out of the cast in a month.

Nick's cough is gone, but now he has fluid in his ears. The pediatrician refers him to an ear, nose, and throat specialist who recommends tubes be put in Nick's ears to drain the fluid. He says this will help his hearing and speech.

How I wish Lisa were here! She'd be able to help me understand that undergoing surgery is the best thing for Nick, and I shouldn't worry. In my mind, I hear her voice explaining, cajoling, lifting the weight of concern off my shoulders. She was good at that.

⚓

The boys are deciding how they want to dress up for Halloween. Victor wants to be the Red Ranger of the "Mighty Morphin Power Rangers." Nick is still undecided but eventually settles on a Transformer, a monster that turns, or transforms, into something else. They will wear these costumes during the school's costume parade as well as the night of trick-or-treating in the neighborhood.

Lisa and I used to love Halloween. We would dress the kids up and one of us would take them out for candy while the other stayed at the house to dole out treats to the other little ghosts and goblins. Recalling this sparks memories of Lisa's fun-loving Halloween costumes. Lisa always chose to dress up as something whimsical and animated — a jack-in-the-box, a chick bursting from an egg — while I usually went for a transformation, morphing myself into 6'6" giant or a creature from another planet.

⚓

Virginie's year is almost up. In November, she will tour the U.S. for three weeks before leaving for France. Immigration law dictates that she stay out of the country for at least three months, but she tells me she would be willing to come back next year if she cannot get a job in France. I know I can always apply for another nanny, but I decide to wait and hope Virginie can return to work for us again. I have found her to be a great help with the kids by giving me free time to grieve or, on bad days, just lie around. She is caring, intelligent, trustworthy, and I know I can depend on her.

Virginie will leave in November when the boys and I go to Massachusetts for Thanksgiving. Once up north, we'll be able to spend time with friends and family. At Christmas, my family will travel to Naples. They will help me with the boys for a couple of weeks, then I will have no help for three months until Virginie returns or I get a new nanny. I believe I can handle it for a little while, so I don't panic.

⚓

It is early November and Nicholas's sixth birthday. We invite a few people over for cake and a subdued celebration. I still have trouble getting excited about birthdays when Lisa is missing them.

"Good night, Nick," I say as I put him to bed.

"You know what?"

"No, what?"

"Mom was at my fourth birthday. She was in the hospital on my fifth birthday, and she was dead for my sixth birthday."

"That's right." I hug Nick tightly.

I am stunned by his insight and how he is trying to comprehend his reality. He is putting his mother's death into terms he can understand. I am saddened every time I look at Nick and Victor and imagine what it must be like to have no mother. I still have my wonderful mother. What is it like for them? Later that night, I tiptoe back into their room and watch them sleep.

⚓

I know I'm supposed to talk to my therapist, but I don't want to today. I sit looking at her, and she waits patiently for me to open up and share my thoughts and feelings. I want to leave. I want to jump up and scream or throw furniture around, and I can't pinpoint why. I just know that today I can't stand being in her office, and I can't stand myself.

I thought I was ready for therapy, and this is another unexpected reaction. A counselor at hospice told me this might happen, so maybe it isn't really unexpected. I can almost laugh at how illogical this is.

⚓

Virginie is off on her U.S. vacation with other people her own age. The day before Thanksgiving, the boys and I fly to Boston. It's a rainy Wednesday night. We take the courtesy shuttle to the rental car office, get into our car, and drive to the exit. Due to the "Big Dig," a ten-year road construction project in Boston, all of the roads surrounding the airport are torn up, and we arrive in Leominster much later than planned.

On Thanksgiving, I drive the boys and Carl to my parents' home in Waltham. The drive on Route 2 takes us past Emerson Hospital. I see flashes of Lisa working as a nurse, the kids being born, and Lisa's death. Suddenly, I want to take a different route to Mom and Dad's house. I want to delay getting there. It's not the house or my parents that I don't want to see; it is the memories of last year's Thanksgiving that I want to avoid. But I know I can't.

⚓

Last Thanksgiving was the last time Lisa left the hospital under her own power. We had gone to Mom and Dad's house. She had worn a new pink sweatsuit and a medicine pump.

"Look at this," she said, lifting the portable medicine pump she was attached to. Just as a nurse would, she explained that the pump enabled her to have a continuous flow of pain reliever.

The mood was neither festive nor depressing. Lisa was upbeat, and we had a good dinner. Lisa ate only a little. I was happy. I thought if she could eat, she must be doing better.

After a while it was time for me to take her back to the hospital. It was just the two of us, and I, not wanting to rush back, drove Big Blue through Concord.

"Can you pull over?" Lisa asked. "I'm going to be sick."

I maneuvered the car near a field of withered, brown weeds. As I stood by her side, she opened the door and threw up.

I didn't want to believe that she was not getting better. I didn't know what to do but rub her back and deny the seriousness of her sickness.

⚓

This Thanksgiving, I am sedate for most of the day. I reflect upon the fact that I have been quiet in general, and I admit to myself that I need to work on overcoming my silence. The boys aren't having any problem being their usual energetic selves.

The Thanksgiving weekend rushes by, and we head back to Florida.

⚓

It's hard to get into the mood of the holiday season in Naples when it isn't cold or threatening snow like up north. I decide it's time to put up the Christmas decorations anyway. It's not exciting, but I'm trying to make this Christmas happier than last year's. I put up the decorations we had in Massachusetts — green garland with a few red ribbons. Once finished, I stand back to see how the house looks, and I can barely see the decorations. The lawn, the bushes and the garland are green, and the house is a light brown. Too much green! I miss Massachusetts. The decorations looked so much better up there, contrasted against the muted colors of winter.

⚓

The adult education classes are starting again, and I sign up for a writing class. It is mostly a review of what I already know. The good part is that the teacher is an author, and it is a bonus having her review my writing and suggest markets.

⚓

Nick likes to fall when he plays soccer at school; it adds to the drama of the sport, I suppose. His knees come home dirty and bruised. I look at his wounded knees and cringe. But Nick doesn't complain. It seems like I'm the only one who whines and complains. And I'm supposed to be the grownup!

⚓

Amazingly, another part of me seems to have broken through the surface of my grief, like a bubble coming to the surface of a once-frozen lake. It's my love of music, which has been dormant.

I started taking trumpet lessons when I was 12. My first major in college was music. At different times I've played trumpet, guitar, and piano, and I also learned to play the flute, violin, and bass clarinet. Making music has always been a part of my life.

For six months or more after Lisa's death, I couldn't listen to music.

I would drive around town in silence. The country music of love and loss was too sad to listen to, and the rock music I grew up with didn't energize me anymore.

But now, I yearn to have music back in my life. At a local pawn store I buy an acoustic guitar for myself and two, half-size acoustic guitars for the kids.

At night after putting the kids to bed, I sit out in the hall so they can hear me play the guitar. I play for half an hour, figuring they will feel safe knowing I am here and hoping they might like the music. After 30 minutes of playing, they are asleep. I go clean the kitchen, pick up the house, and do general housework. I like routines.

One night as I'm strumming a familiar tune, Nick calls to me.

"Dad?"

"Yes, Nick."

"Can you stop playing so we can get to sleep?"

I put the guitar down and walk back to my room. Then I chuckle to myself as I think what courage it must have taken for him to speak up.

I'm glad the boys are self-assured enough to tell me things like that. From now on, I'll practice the guitar in my room.

16

Milestone

December 1994. One year without Lisa. Tomorrow is the first anniversary of Lisa's death. I miss talking to her, looking at her, cuddling in bed with her, and dancing with her. I miss her smile, and the look in her eyes that said I was special. It makes me long to have a partner and a good friend again.

But if I find someone, what if they die on me, too? I know it's an irrational fear to worry that the new person I'm going to be with will die, but I think it, nonetheless. I should date women who are ten years younger than I am so I don't have to see them die, yet I know age is not a guarantee.

The pain of missing her is not as overwhelming as last year. I am not as numb. It's more like a longing than a traumatic loss.

⚓

At the office, Sue suggests I treat myself to a better car. My Acura suits me just fine, but I follow through on Sue's suggestion and drive to a Mercedes dealership in Fort Lauderdale.

Because of my frugal upbringing, I can't bring myself to choose one of the new models. Instead, I buy a six-year-old Mercedes sportster that seems more affordable. Frugality wins out over status.

I take possession of the Mercedes on the one-year anniversary of Lisa's death. Am I trying to fill a hole inside of me? Or did Sue suggest I treat myself as a distraction from my grief? Perhaps, I decide, I am changing, and change is good.

I have survived this first year of widowerhood. I feel proud. I can smile. Through my volunteer efforts, people at Seacrest know me. They stop to greet me, making me feel that I'm part of an extended family at the boys' school.

It has been a year of hard work: moving to a new state; finding Julia a good home; getting the boys to school; learning to be the decision-maker; dealing with Lisa's estate; and accepting responsibility for everything.

Each day is no longer a first of its kind. I've lived through those first days, survived them, and I am ready to move on to the next phase of my grief recovery work.

⚓

Virginie is back from her three-week trip to the western U.S., and she has 29 rolls of film to be developed. In only a couple of days, she will fly back to France.

As I sit down to write her a letter of thanks, my emotions pour out and I realize how much I care for her. She has been a bright light to me, Victor, and Nick, and I know we will all miss her.

We arrive at the airport and walk Virginie to her gate. The boys say goodbye. I give her a long hug, we separate and look at each other with tear-filled eyes. I nod to her and she nods back as we acknowledge that we care for each other, not as male/female, but as family. The experience of Lisa's passing has created a unique bond, and I know she'll be back to help all of us.

⚓

My parents, brothers, sister, and Carl travel to Naples for our first Christmas in Florida.

The boys are excited to open their presents, yet they wait for me to get up before they rip their packages open. It's so different — instead of snow, we can frolic on the beach on Christmas. Even though I'm not overjoyed with having to open gifts, I accept my situation better than I did last Christmas morning. I light candles in memory of Lisa and place them on a side table.

A week later, the boys and I head to Massachusetts for the last week of Christmas vacation. The rest of the family stays in Naples.

Over New Year's, I walk around the Leominster house, and the memories wash over me. Everything about the two of us happened in Leominster, and everything is still here. When we bought the house in Naples we bought new furniture. All of Lisa's belongings stayed in Leominster. Nothing of hers was sent to Florida with my stuff. Did she realize something I didn't?

⚓

We arrive back in Naples after the new year, and I have a panic attack. I break out in a cold sweat as I relentlessly pace the floor. Leominster represents my married life, my life as part of a couple. Naples represents my single life, my life as a widower, and all the grief. We wanted Naples to be ours, too, but that will never be. I feel so alone. I miss Lisa so much.

⚓

Ray, my friend with whom I joined the gym, has invited me to the Kiwanis Club of North Naples. I like the people in the club, so I decide to apply for membership. It's time to stretch myself and reach out to others.

⚓

In early January 1995, while sitting in my M.C. Johnson Co. office, I start to feel light-headed and nauseated. The left side of my face tingles. I lay my head on the desk and take a cat nap, hoping the strangeness will go away. When I wake up, my left jaw is numb.

I feel a sharp jab in my left shoulder. Could it be a heart attack? A stroke? I try not to panic. I walk quickly to the warehouse to find Joe.

"Hey, Joe," I call out.

"What's up, Rich?"

"Could you drive me to the hospital?"

"Sure," agrees Joe, concern in his voice. "Are you feeling okay?"

"Feel kind of funny."

Joe drives me to the emergency room. I'm convinced I'm having a heart attack. The doctors hook up monitors, ask me questions, and give me a pill to put under my tongue. They decide to keep me overnight, and I wear a heart monitor all night.

Nick didn't want to come see me in the hospital. I can't blame him. Victor came to see me, even though he was nervous. Their most recent memory of the hospital was when their mother was there, and she died. When the boys visited Lisa in the hospital, they would lie in her bed and watch TV. They, too, must have been ignoring her declining health.

In the morning, a neurologist comes to see me and puts me through some tests. He tells me the good news: I didn't have a heart attack or a small stroke. I'm relieved.

The word "stroke" scares me. My father had suffered a stroke, which paralyzed his left side. Because of a family predisposition to strokes, I'm told to take an aspirin a day for the rest of my life. The symptoms that I thought were from a heart attack are actually diagnosed as skeletal muscular problems in my shoulder and neck. My prognosis is excellent. An aspirin a day won't be tough to handle. A few days after the hospital stay, I undergo a stress test and find that my heart is strong. Looks like the boys won't be orphaned after all. I am relieved. The thought of tragedy striking the boys again would have been too much to bear.

⚓

I attend my last hospice meeting in January. It has been a year, and I'm aware of how much I've learned and grown. The last couple of grief sessions have been difficult because there are new people with fresh sorrow. I can feel their anguish, and I don't want to go back to the pain and grief that I've already lived through. It was a crushing, searing pain, and I am ready to move on to the next step. I decide to join the "Life After Grief" group held at Jewish Family Services, an arm of the Jewish Federation of Collier County.

⚓

It's the end of January and time to remember Lisa's birthday. I buy a cake for the boys to celebrate the day, and I buy plane tickets to Massachusetts. We are going north for a weekend. I need to see my friends; I need to feel connected. And it will be good for Victor and Nick to visit with our northern family and friends.

⚓

Life is feeling like life again. For the past year, it's as though life was making decisions for me, and now I am making decisions for my life. It's my way of trying to control where my life is going. I have been reacting to what happened; now I want to make things happen.

The boys are doing well in school. They have finished their bereavement therapy, and their therapist, Ms. Susan, feels they have dealt with their grief in healthy ways. They no longer need to see her every week. She says kids deal with grief a little at a time, and as they grow older, they'll understand more and have more questions. They are not like adults, who try to tackle it all at once.

⚓

The kids and I can get along great one minute, and the next minute we are each other's worst nightmare. I like being a parent, even with all its challenges, but I certainly miss Virginie. She made my day-to-day life so much easier.

I receive a letter from her, telling me she will be back next month. I can do this by myself until then, I think. At least it's a good test to see if I can. The hardest household task is deciding what to cook for dinner. I used to love cooking and preparing meals, and now I have to plan meals when nothing appeals to my appetite. If I don't plan, then I won't have food in the house, and it seems the kids are eating everything except the dinners I create.

I try to cook good, nutritious meals, and all they want is junk food. Nick just stares at the chicken and broccoli I've prepared and turns up his nose. But that's Nick; he's been a picky eater since he was a toddler.

⚓

In February, my parents arrive for a visit so they can watch the kids as Phil and I head off to Atlanta for the Critical Care Nurses Show. At our exhibit booth, we are on our feet for six hours a day as we promote and demonstrate Cath-Secure and try to increase our sales. The response to the product is good. This nursing show is emotionally easier for me than the last one. The medical equipment doesn't seem to dredge up painful memories of Lisa's illness and death. This is encouraging.

One afternoon at the booth, as I am telling a group of nurses about our products, I suddenly feel very light-headed. It reminds me of the time I went to the emergency room. I'm scared. I don't want to have a stroke. I sit down and have a drink of soda. Five minutes later I feel fine.

⚓

That night after dinner, I relax in my room and decide to watch an in-room movie. If Lisa were here, she'd choose a comedy, like *Monty Python* or *National Lampoon*. She loved comedies, and we enjoyed watching the weekly television show "Moonlighting," where Bruce Willis and Cybill Shepherd play lighthearted detectives.

The hotel's offerings don't include a decent comedy, so I choose *Sleepless in Seattle,* starring Tom Hanks, one of my favorite actors. The film opens in a cemetery where the wife who has died of cancer is being buried. She leaves behind her husband and son. The husband decides to relocate and start a new life.

I groan. This is just like my life, and I'm tempted to hit the "off" button on the remote control. Then the movie jumps ahead 18 months, and the rest of the story unfolds. It ends with Tom Hanks finding happiness and a new love.

It has been 13 months since Lisa died, and I don't see how I could ever be that happy and in love only five months from now. As I watch the movie, memories of what I had and what will never be surge through me. I go through a box of tissues as I dab at my eyes. The movie ends, I turn off the lights, close my eyes, and lie face down on the bed.

As I drift off to sleep, an outline of Lisa appears in my vision. It's a reddish outline of her body, and she's in front of me, facing me. Her arms embrace me. I feel my imaginary body close to her, and wrap my arms around her, too. We fit just as if we're embracing in real life. It's so real that I accept it. I know she isn't physically here, so it must be her spirit body. It feels like her. I'm holding her again, and I feel so whole and fulfilled because she is in my arms once more. I fall asleep blissfully.

17

Possibilities

March 1995. Fifteen months without Lisa. The first Sunday in March, the memories of our wedding anniversary cause a grief attack. I want to run away. I need to escape the cascade of grief that threatens to suffocate me. I drive over to Sue and Joe's house.

"Would you like something to drink?" Sue offers.

"Yes, I'll have a beer." It's only 10:00 a.m.

I drink the beer and talk. Joe offers me another alcoholic beverage, and I drink a few shots of Sambuca. I talk, laugh, cry, and drink. I have succeeded in chasing the demons away — at least for the short term. The alcohol catches up with me, and I need to lie down. Sue and Joe offer their couch, and I sleep for three hours.

When I wake around 2:00 p.m., my head is pounding, but I must drive home. It's a good thing that Mom and Dad have come to visit so they can watch the kids. It takes three days before my head feels better, and I spend much of that time lying flat on my back because it hurts too much to move my head.

I'm glad I don't like alcohol because it would be too easy to try to drink my grief away.

⚓

It is now March and Virginie is back. What a relief! It is so good to see her and to have her back in our family. Our deep feelings for each other are still evident, yet we keep a professional distance.

⚓

I have started the Life After Grief group at the Jewish Family Services. Janet heads the group. I see some familiar faces from hospice. The structure of the group is that we meet four weeks in a row then take two weeks off so we don't get too dependent on the group.

There is a tendency to depend on groups because they provide a safe haven, a place where people share the same experiences without judgment from the others. One of the men there is dependent upon groups, even though he says he isn't. He attends five meetings a week, and he says everything is okay with him. I look into his eyes, and I see things are not okay. He is struggling because he doesn't want to come to grips with what happened.

I am young enough to be his son. I remind myself that age doesn't automatically bring wisdom. He has to work at it. So do I.

We have to live our lives ourselves, and I know I am coming to grips with my reality. How far I am coming, I don't know. I still slog through many days when I feel like it is day one; I can't eat, I can't sleep, and I hurt so much I don't even want to be alive.

Yet most of the days are free from the intense torment of the first year. I feel that things are returning to a normal point, where normal is lonely, coupled with the stress of single parenthood.

⚓

I go to Nick's kindergarten class and read stories to the kids. Nick's teacher shows me a picture Nick drew called "The Flying Pickle." Seeing the picture sparks a memory of when the boys, my friend Ray, and I made up a story called "The Floor Pickle" while eating dinner at a local restaurant.

Nick's picture inspires me to write a children's story about the pickle, which I read to both Nick and Victor's classes. The schoolchildren like the story so much they ask me to read it again and again. Imagine! I've written something that readers find entertaining. Perhaps I should send the story out for publication.

⚓

I join Kiwanis, and as a social get-together, the club plays golf once a week. I am a terrible golfer; I take nine shots to accomplish what everyone else does in three or four. So I just keep laughing at myself and try to hit the ball as far as I can. Surprisingly, I usually do well on the last hole. At least I am getting out with people so I can learn to relate to others who have not been through what I have survived.

⚓

Life is lonely. I want to be in a relationship, but I still feel an unshakable fear that the person I get involved with will die. I know it probably won't happen that way, but that fear is in me. I am also afraid of how much I need somebody. I don't want a relationship, yet I need someone to help me feel alive.

I get together with a widow I've met, and we give each other back massages. She does most of the touching, and it is a physical pleasure that tells me I'm still alive. I wish the anguish of healing would be over so I can live my life and feel like I did before.

I'm trying to enjoy life to the best of my ability, but I often feel overwhelmed. Everything is frustrating. Sometimes it seems I can't do anything right. I am a lousy writer; I don't take care of the kids well; I can't cook; I look horrible; and the house is a mess.

The other day I jumped on my bike and rode as hard as I could for as long as I could. The flatness of the south Florida roads is not challenging, but I pedaled feverishly, trying to escape my life. Except there is no escape. It is what it is, and I have to accept it and carry on.

⚓

In April, Phil and I travel to the oncology show in Anaheim, California. I get in touch with a family friend whose parents are still in Massachusetts and are good friends with my parents. It's his bowling night, and I go with him and his wife to watch them bowl. It's good to make contact with him.

The next month we are off to the critical care show in New Orleans. When I return, I will take the boys and fly north to surprise my dad on his 75th birthday.

⚓

An opportunity has opened up. The Kiwanis Club needs a volunteer newsletter editor, so I take the position. I figure it will get me writing again on a regular basis and provide me with some focus. I have trouble concentrating on freelance writing when the reality of life without Lisa is still pounding me in the face.

However, even with all the frustration and loneliness, I can still see the possibilities in life. It's amazing. One day I'm huddled in my bed not wanting to face the world, and the next day I can conquer it all. I think I have turned a corner. I can actually see days that are brighter, and I can accept the challenging days.

The majority of the time I feel as if I simply exist. I know that I want to write again, so writing the Kiwanis newsletter should help get me back into the rhythm of writing, and it does. Now I'm writing, getting out with people, and all in all, moving in a positive direction. Nonetheless, I will be glad when summer comes, and I can go up north again.

⚓

In the Life After Grief group, we discuss dating. Dating? Yes, it is something I want to do, but who would want me? I'm a whole lot better than a year ago, but I still feel incomplete and damaged.

I did have a date recently. I took Elizabeth, the office manager from the pediatrician's office, out for lunch one Saturday. I put the top down on the Mercedes and drove to Marco Island. It was fun having lunch with a friend.

⚓

Sue has invited me to her daughter's wedding in Naples. I have known Sue's family for 15 years, and I admire her daughter Erica's courage. She suffers from Crohn's disease and is constantly in and out of the hospital, yet she never complains. It feels good for me to have someone other than myself and the kids to care about. I became so fixated on Lisa's disease and death that I was unable to reach out to others and lend them a helping hand.

At Erica and Danny's pre-wedding dinner, they surprise me by making a toast to me for helping them. I don't feel that I did very much for them. But they are grateful that I rented my Naples condo to them at such a low price and helped Erica buy my Acura when I bought my Mercedes.

For several reasons, I decide to bring a date to the wedding. I have to get used to the idea of being seen with someone other than Lisa, and my family and friends have to get used to the idea, too. I ask Elizabeth to go with me.

My parents and Carl fly south for the wedding. Victor and Nicholas are in the wedding as ring bearers, and they look cute in their little tuxedos. I think back to the day Lisa and I were wed.

I affectionately called it the double-handicap wedding. My father was my best man, and because he had suffered a stroke the year before, he hobbled down the aisle leaning on a four-prong cane. The day before the wedding, Carl, an amputee, slipped on the ice and broke the kneecap of his right stump. He couldn't wear his prosthetic device, but he was determined to walk Lisa down the aisle. Using crutches, he did.

For a few minutes, it was even a triple-handicap wedding. My knees shook so much I thought I'd fall down. Then I saw my beautiful bride and knew this marriage was so right. My knees stopped shaking.

During the reception when the band played our wedding song, I thought I was in heaven, embracing the woman of my dreams. As Anne Murray's pop vocals filled the hall, Lisa and I whispered the words to each other, as we had done dozens of times: "Could I have this dance for the rest of my life? Would you be my partner every night? When we're together it feels so right. Could I have this dance for the rest of my life?"

At Erica's reception, Elizabeth and I sit at a table with the boys, my parents, and Carl. I think this is the first time that my parents, and especially Carl, have seen me with someone other than Lisa. I'm glad to have someone to dance with and talk to, even if it is a little awkward for all of us.

⚓

Before I know it, June is here and the first year of school has ended. The boys, Virginie, and I fly to Massachusetts for the summer. My life without Lisa has now totaled 17 months.

In my bedroom, I wander around and look at all of Lisa's clothing and the items she kept in the room. I open each drawer of her dresser, and realize — for the umpteenth time — she will never wear the lingerie, socks, sweaters, and blouses. Last year I couldn't clean out her pocketbooks, but this year I will try again to sort through her belongings. I begin by throwing away stuff — mostly papers — that don't connect me with her.

I clean out Lisa's pocketbooks and throw them away. Even though they still have significance, the emotional tie seems less intense, and I don't experience the gut-wrenching torment that knocked me down last year. I also discard all her panties and bras, except one bra, which I put in the closet with all her sweaters and dresses. I'm not sure why I keep the bra, except that it reminds me of the woman she was.

I look at the other clothes in the closet, and memories fill the room. I can visualize Lisa wearing each outfit, see her broad smile and hear her infectious laughter. I know that some day the clothes will just be clothes; but for now, Lisa's essence remains. And for now, so will the clothing.

Throughout the huge house in Leominster, so much of Lisa's personality is still alive. The books she read line the bookcase in the living room. Even before her cancer diagnosis, she was an avid spiritual seeker, reading leading-edge authors like Deepak Chopra. After we married, we took part in an intensive workshop based on the spiritual text, *A Course in Miracles*. During her illness, Lisa became passionate about reading every book published on holistic healing and other nonconventional philosophies. We even traveled to Sedona, Arizona, because Lisa had read a book about the healing energy vortexes found at sacred sites there.

Self-help books fill almost every shelf, but then my eye spots a row of fictional works. The quick-read stories by pulp authors such as Danielle Steele gave Lisa a much-needed respite from day-to-day stresses and responsibilities. She'd curl up in bed with one of these novels and read for hours, oblivious to the happenings around her.

Surrounded by her clothes, books, and even her taste in color and décor — the mauve hues, antique mirrors and dolls she loved to collect and display — I don't feel the grief and depression of last year. I just feel sad that Lisa is not here to enjoy everything with me and the boys.

⚓

Romantically, there is really no one in my life. This second year of life without Lisa has been a year of loneliness.

I still want someone in my life on a relationship level, yet I can't bring myself to get involved with anyone. There is Donna, whom I see from time to time in the summer. We have been intimate, but she wants me more than I want her. I need closeness and intimacy, but the timing isn't right. Elizabeth and I enjoyed several dates, but I haven't called her in months.

I know I still have much healing to do. I feel I've been rejected by Lisa. I know it's not rational to feel Lisa rejected me when she died, but it's the way I honestly feel. I need to deal with this and work through more aspects of my grief recovery.

Waiting is hard, but I would rather be alone than begin a relationship just for the sake of having a relationship. I tell myself that it takes time to adjust, grow, and heal, although sometimes my progress seems too slow. I wish the pain would end so I can move ahead. I know there are phases I must pass through, and this one is frustrating. I realize, though, that this phase is preparing me for the next chapter of my life.

⚓

The boys, Virginie, and I visit the Lost River in New Hampshire. It's a river that runs through and under granite boulders. I remember a little about it from when I was a kid. The boys and I crawl through the tight spaces. Virginie comes with us under rocks and through crevices. We also visit the Flume, and then we stop at a restaurant for dinner. I sit next to Virginie, and the boys sit on the other side of the table. The waiter comes to take our order. The boys tell him what they'd like to eat, and the waiter turns to Virginie to make sure it's okay with their "mom."

When the waiter walks away, Virginie and I look at each other and laugh. She has been mistaken for my wife many times. It used to bother her because at age 25, she felt she was too young to have school-age children. Now, because we have both grown, she and I can chuckle.

⚓

This month, Victor is turning eight, and Virginie will leave us for the second time. I can't thank her enough for what she has brought to our lives. I don't want her to go; I want her to stay with us. While I know she needs to return to her life in France and have fun with friends like any normal young woman in her twenties, I still hope she will tell me she wants to stay with us.

It is late June in Leominster. We are having dinner, and the kids are acting up. Virginie is getting upset.

"It's okay," I say, placing my hand on her arm.

I know I am going to miss her. But I will always remember her smile and the small inhalation sound she makes sometimes before she speaks.

⚓

The rest of the summer, without Virginie, isn't as difficult as I thought it would be. As I look toward the fall, with the boys in school, I'll only need someone for a couple of nights and weekends. I realize I have grown enough that I can handle single-parenting. I decide not to hire another nanny.

This turns out to be a wise decision, because my older sister, Stephanie, has decided to move to Naples, and she says she will help me with the boys for the next year. This is great! What wonderful serendipity!

I will have my sister with me; the boys will have their aunt. Stephanie will help all of us. Family closeness has been an important part of my life. I grew up with 40 cousins and 20 aunts and uncles. The families were always getting together. My boys have five aunts and uncles and two cousins. Now they will have their Aunt Stephanie with them.

At a party at Mom's house, Steph tells her plans to Claudia, our cousin. Claudia and I exchange a knowing glance because we understand what it's like to raise children. Steph doesn't have kids. What an awakening she's going to have!

⚓

Before we leave New England, Victor, Nick, Carl and I travel to visit Julia in her new home. I has been over a year since we've seen her, and we talk about how much Julia has probably grown. She was only 10 months old when we last saw her.

We are warmly ushered into the den by her parents. The door suddenly opens and two giggling toddlers come running in and hop onto their parents' laps. It is Julia and her brother. What a shock! Here's sweet little Julia, walking and even talking! She doesn't even seem to recognize me, and I start to laugh. I laugh at my own stifled imagination and the new reality. I laugh because Julia is their child, she is happy, and I am so very glad for her.

Summer is over, and I close the doors to our rooms in Leominster. Lisa's clothes still hang in the closet. Steph, the boys, and I head back to Naples for the start of another school year. It's only August 12, and I feel I didn't have enough time in Leominster to ever feel fully settled and ready to say goodbye. But we must return to Naples in time for the boys to get their school supplies and be ready for the first day of school at the end of August.

Forward Motion

September 1995. Twenty months without Lisa. We arrive back in Naples, and I see that the house next to mine is for sale. I decide to buy it so my parents and Carl can stay there when they visit us. I call it our guesthouse.

Steph is adjusting to the area. She has the front bedroom, the one with the private bath; I still use the back room, or recreation room, as my bedroom. The kids have the two rooms next to each other. Steph is learning what it's like to be around kids!

The boys start their second year at Seacrest. Victor has Mrs. Maxwell for second grade, and Nick has Miss Southwick for first grade. They seem like wonderful teachers, and I think the boys will have another good school year.

⚓

My friend Trish has come down for a visit. Recently, her live-in boyfriend was killed in a motorcycle accident, and I can see the depths of her loss and anger. I show Trish the wall that separates the small den from the kitchen. I have removed the cabinets on the kitchen side, because I'm about to tear down the wall and bring light into the room.

"Here, try this," I offer, giving Trish a hammer. "You can pound the wall right here."

She takes the hammer and pounds on the wall. As it breaks, sheet-rock goes flying. Trish batters away until she creates a hole three feet in diameter, then stands back to admire her destruction. "That felt great."

We agree it's a good way to release some of the anger of grief.

After she leaves, I take the Sawzall and begin cutting until the wall pops down. Without that wall, the house looks much brighter. It's such an improvement that I wish I'd done it sooner.

⚓

I'm beginning to hate this house. The roof is starting to leak, and there are bugs in the ceiling. I discover that the electric wiring, where Trish broke the wall, is very old and wasn't installed correctly. It's a fire hazard. Even after taking the wallpaper off, removing the rugs, and painting the walls, the house is too dark. I feel depressed just walking into it.

I don't know whether to sell the house and move, or have the house renovated. I find it hard to make a decision, and I don't want to make any decisions right now. I have a trade show to attend in San Francisco.

⚓

It's October; Steph and the boys join me in San Francisco. While Joe and I work the trade show, Steph and the kids see the wondrous sights of the city. After the three-day show ends, Joe heads back to Naples.

I rent a car, and Steph, the boys, and I drive inland to Angel's Camp, California. This is where Mark Twain wrote about the jumping-frog contest. We are here to visit California Caverns and Moaning Caverns. We then tour Big Tree State Park and marvel at the giant sequoia trees.

The contrast between the dark rocky caves and the towering trees is wonderful. I love it. And I love traveling to interesting places with Victor and Nicholas. They are fun to be with and continue to give me two solid reasons to embrace life with gusto.

⚓

My euphoria from the trip is short lived. Once home again in Naples, I find I can't stand the house. Within the first week, I decide to move into a house I bought as an investment in Golden Gate Estates. It's not being rented right now, so we might as well live there. I figure the move will help me decide whether to remodel or sell the Fourth Avenue home.

Golden Gate Estates is located within the general Naples area, yet it features large multiple-acre lots. Ours is filled with pine trees, reminding me somewhat of New Hampshire. The house itself has a country feel to it. It is bright and airy with a large kitchen. The boys love the pool. Steph moves into the little guest cottage out back. I have the master bedroom with its large, luxurious bathroom. The walk-in closet is big enough for my office. French doors lead from my bedroom to the screened-in porch area, which here in Florida we call a "lanai." The boys each have a bedroom on opposite sides of the house.

We have been in the Estates for one week, and already I miss living in a neighborhood. When I was a kid, I could walk right over to a friend's house or even to the local store. Out here in the Estates, there is nowhere to go. I feel more isolated here than I did on Fourth Avenue downtown. This isn't good. I need to be around people.

"I've made my decision," I say to the boys. "I'm going to remodel the house on Fourth Avenue; then we'll move back." They take the news in stride.

I contact a contractor friend from my Kiwanis club, and we talk about remodeling the house. I decide that the three separate levels of roof have to go. The house will be covered with one new roof. We'll vault the ceilings and combine the kitchen, laundry area, and den into one room that will become the large eat-in kitchen. It will open right into the dining room.

The work begins. How long it will take is anyone's guess.

⚓

It's Thanksgiving, and we're creating a tradition by flying north to Leominster for the weekend, just like last year. I'm again aware of how fortunate I am to be able to afford to hop on a plane for a holiday weekend. When we arrive, I visit the cemetery alone, where I cry and yell at Lisa for leaving me. It's a brief railing against my fate and hers. It's still a better Thanksgiving than last year. My crying jags are becoming fewer and less intense. Maybe I've reached another turning point.

⚓

When we get back from Thanksgiving, the boys and I start decorating the Estates house for Christmas. We put the tree next to the brick fireplace in the family room, and a happy, festive atmosphere fills our home.

I feel a grief attack approaching as I open a box of handmade holiday crafts Lisa made through the years. I suggest to the boys that they decide where to place each item. Crafting was one of Lisa's hobbies, and the boys unpack box after box of her creations. From sparkling stars to adorn the tree to folksy wreaths to hang on each door, Lisa's handiwork brings warmth and charm. The grief attack passes, and instead of cringing each time I look at one of her crafts, I'm able to be with the memory of when she created it. I can see her sitting at the kitchen table, hunched over a pile of pine cones, ribbon, glitter, and glue.

My parents and Carl have arrived from Massachusetts and are staying at the Fourth Avenue guesthouse because workers are hard at work ripping the roof off the Fourth Avenue main house. I buy presents, fill stockings, and get ready for Christmas morning when we open gifts. I set up the camera and take a shot of us wearing paper Santa hats. Christmas does seem happy this year.

⚓

Friends from Kiwanis invite me out for New Year's Eve, and they arrange for me to have a blind date. I don't feel too strange not knowing my date, and I am able to have a good time. But New Year's Day I wake up in a foul mood. I had fun last night; I didn't think of death or dying. But now that I'm back to my real life, I find it depressing.

Thanks to my counseling sessions, I expect some of these mood swings and am aware of why I'm feeling depressed. I realize I miss the good times, and I know this foul mood was a reaction to the previous carefree and enjoyable evening. While I'm unable to alter my current state, at least I have a better understanding of how events affect me.

⚓

The school year draws to a close, and I am making changes to my life. I have been asked to join the Board of Trustees of Seacrest School. At the end of the school year, I joke with Miss Southwick, and I ask her if she would like to go out sometime when I get back from Leominster. She says yes.

The boys, Steph, and I fly north for the summer.

⚓

We are back in Leominster again to enjoy the summer in Massachusetts and to be with my family and friends. I still need to connect with everybody here. I look into our bedroom closet, and Lisa's dresses and sweaters continue to hang on the right side.

It has been two-and-a-half years since she died. I now feel ready to part with the clothes.

I talk with our neighbor about Lisa's clothes, and she tells me about an organization that gives clothes to women who are going back into the work force but can't afford to buy a new wardrobe.

Lisa was always helping others. I like the idea that her clothes can help other people, especially working women.

I scan all the closets. There are so many clothes to donate — business outfits, casual wear, even some fancy dresses. All of them are on hangers, and some are still in the protective plastic bags from the dry cleaners. I empty out the bedroom closet and a spare closet where Lisa kept other clothes. I have to make three trips to my car as I fill it with Lisa's things.

I drive to the old Price Street School and find the Community Clothes Closet. While I feel good about donating her things, I also feel sad. By removing her stuff, it's almost as if I'm getting rid of Lisa.

My intention is not to get rid of her memory. I realize I will always have that. But finally I understand that I don't want to become attached to symbols or make a memorial to her with her things. Her memory is alive within my mind and heart.

My practical side says these items are just taking up space and will never be used. They will never mean what they did when she was alive.

I am coming to grips with the concept that removing clothing and items that were specific and special to her is not a sign of disrespect. I want to move into a new life beyond her. She is dead and buried, no matter how much that thought hurts me. I am only 42, and I want to live again and love again.

⚓

The summer slips by, and we are back in Florida. The school year brings changes for us all. I start my volunteer work as a member of the Board of Trustees at Seacrest Country Day School, and Steph gets a regular job.

Victor's third grade class is studying about inventors, and I am invited to visit the class to talk about Lisa and her invention, Cath-Secure. As I get dressed and ready to go, I hurriedly put on my socks and shoes. But my right foot feels uncomfortable, like something is wedged in the toe of my sock. I am amazed to find a shiny penny. As I read the year inscribed on the coin — 1993 — I smile and whisper a prayer of gratitude. That was the year Lisa died. Surely, this 1993 penny is a tangible sign that Lisa's love is still with me and the boys.

My talk to Victor's class goes extremely well. The students are impressed that Victor's mom was an inventor. They are also shocked to learn that his mom is dead.

⚓

As the boys get older, the need for volunteers in the classroom decreases, so I spend less time at school. The school year whizzes by. I don't know where the time goes, but it's gone.

Miss Southwick and I go out to Kiwanis functions and movies. She is sweet. I only kissed her once, as I find it is hard to distinguish between her as a woman and as a teacher at the boys' school. My mind isn't flexible enough to make that shift.

Another step forward: I discover I can ask women out, and it seems normal to do so.

Remembrance Season

November 1996. Three years without Lisa. Nick still asks me if I am going to get married. I tell him yes, I would like to some day, but it would happen way into the future. I don't really think of myself as "single," the way men might who never had a wife. I think of myself as "temporarily un-married."

The new school year is well under way, and I am now Secretary of the Board of Trustees at the boys' school.

Nick is having problems with ear infections, so last week he underwent surgery to have tubes put in his ears again. I feel like a bad father today because Nick told me twice that his ear was draining, and I was impatient with him. I'm burned out today.

Day after day it is the same drudgery: do laundry, cook meals, clean the bathroom. When will the kids learn to pick up the toilet seat before they pee? I'm aggravated and frustrated. I wish I were married again and that Lisa were here. She was always on top of everything.

⚓

Now that it is November, I start to get into the remembrance season. Four years ago she was in the hospital. Soon it will be Thanksgiving, and I'll remember taking Lisa to my parents' house for dinner, even though she had no appetite and what she did manage to eat came up on the way back to the hospital.

I didn't consciously admit how ill she was. I never talked to the doctors. I didn't seek them out because Lisa kept me informed of what the doctors told her about the cancer and her treatments. I was as much in denial of her condition as she was.

I couldn't see my denial, but all that ended swiftly with one phone call. It was just after Thanksgiving in 1993 when Lisa's sister Bonda called the hospital from her home in California. Lisa was out of her hospital room for a medical diagnostic test, and Sue, Joe, and I were in the room. The phone rang, and I answered it.

"What's the story?" Bonda asked. "Dad says Lisa is doing okay, but Judy says Lisa won't live until Christmas."

The hairs on the back of my neck stood up.

"That's the first I've heard that," I said. "I'll check around."

I hung up the phone. What was she talking about? Something wasn't right, and I needed to find some answers. Why would Lisa's friend Judy say that? I left the hospital room to find Lisa's doctors and, near the nurses' station, ran into the surgeon who had helped during her last operation. "What is Lisa's prognosis?" I asked.

He looked up from the chart in his hand. "About six months."

I avoided his eyes. Six months? How can that be? I turned around and saw Lisa's oncologist sitting at the nurses' station.

"What is Lisa's prognosis?" I asked him.

"Three or four months, I'd say."

Months? Months, not years, but months? This couldn't be true!

My intestines migrated to my head as I felt that any second I would explode or vomit.

I rushed to Lisa's room and grabbed my jacket. "I need air," I told Sue and Joe. "I'll meet you at the car."

I bolted from the room. I wanted to scream! I couldn't breathe. I wanted to punch a hole in the wall. I wanted to cry, but first I had to get out of the hospital, and I couldn't get out of there fast enough.

I burst into the cold November air. Walking swiftly to the parking garage, I ran up five flights of stairs to the top of the garage where our car was parked. As I looked at the hospital, I kicked the cement wall.

How could Lisa be so sick? She'd gone into the hospital before and come out. This can't be true! A sinking feeling told me that it was true. She hadn't said anything to me, yet the signs of her weakening were right in front of me — the swollen legs, her immobility. I'd ignored them because I had faith in her, complete faith and trust that we would grow old together and watch videotapes of the kids and grandkids.

Sue and Joe arrived at the car. I insisted that I drive — I needed to be in control of something. Joe talked to me the whole way home. I heard him only now and then, and I didn't remember the drive because my mind was still trying to cope and process the insanity that was starting to descend upon me.

I became angry with Lisa. She had been in the hospital for six weeks, and she didn't tell me anything. She kept saying she was going to get better, and I believed her. Now the doctors were saying she wouldn't.

⚓

The thought of talking about death scared me, and I know it scared Lisa, but I had to say something. I needed some guidance from her. One day as we were returning from one of her cigarette breaks, we stepped onto the elevator and I blurted out: "If you die in Florida, what do you want?"

She said a memorial service in Massachusetts would be good.

Asking her that one question was awkward. I felt as if mentioning death would bring it on. I realized that part of her fear was that negative thoughts would turn against her and come true.

It was the only question I could ask her. The rest of what I wanted to say stayed inside me.

⚓

My house has been remodeled in time for Thanksgiving, and we move back in. Now the house feels open and spacious, and when I walk in, I feel my spirits soar. So the house is new, and I'm happy with that, but I'm still frustrated with life. I feel under-appreciated and emotionally tired.

I stare at the calendar and think of various anniversaries. It was four years ago that Lisa had her last Thanksgiving. The day after Thanksgiving is the 12th anniversary of my marriage proposal to her. Five years ago we went to my 20th high school reunion together. My 25th high school reunion is tomorrow, and I will fly to Massachusetts and attend. Alone.

⚓

For the most part I'm happy, but I'm afraid of relationships.

Two years before meeting Lisa, my trust had been broken by a woman I had been dating, and after that I didn't trust anyone — except Lisa.

After four years of life without Lisa, I feel neglected and afraid. I'm afraid to open myself up to be loved. I'm afraid to love someone who may die, or to love the wrong one and get hurt. I'm afraid of how needy I am.

I need to be touched, loved, appreciated, and comforted.

The kids are going through a phase, which I hope will be short-lived! They blame me for everything that is wrong with them, their friends, and their school. Just when I thought things were getting easier in my grief recovery, I find myself sinking to new lows.

⚓

My father's health takes a turn for the worse, so I fly up and down the coast many times in the winter and early spring. I feel so fortunate to be able to afford to travel whenever I want, and I say a silent prayer of thanks to Lisa for making this possible.

I spend time with my dad, telling him how much I love him. I also tell my mom that I love her. It's quite a transformation for me to be saying "I love you" to them. I learned from Lisa's death not to wait to tell someone how much I care.

It's mid-April, and I'm back in Florida when the phone call comes informing me that my father has died. The boys and I travel to Massachusetts for his funeral and to spend some time with my mom.

⚓

When I was 16, I had an awakening in the relationship with my father. As we sat opposite each other one evening at the dinner table, I looked at him and realized for the first time how alike we were. I remember thinking how very much I loved him. From that day forward, we found it easy to communicate about whatever topic came to mind. Our relationship became so comfortable that we could disagree without generating hard feelings.

He worked at the same company for 40 years. Sadly, shortly after he retired, he had a stroke. His retirement dream to drive a pickup truck and be a handyman was dashed. His "stupid side," as he called it, was his left side. He needed a cane to walk and could lift his left arm, but it was pretty much useless.

Twelve years after the first operation the doctors advised him that in order to keep the blood flowing in his carotid arteries he needed surgery to clear the blockage. The operation carried both a benefit and a downside.

The benefit would be that he would remain the same with improved blood flow. But there was a risk that he could suffer another stroke on the operating table. He chose to do nothing for several months before deciding to have the operation last summer. Tragically, a stroke did occur during the surgery, which sent him to a nursing home, where he remained bedridden and unable to talk.

I visited Dad while he was in the nursing home and the hospital. I talked to him and caressed his head or held his hand. We knew he could hear us because his shoulder would jiggle when we told funny stories. Yet his circulation to the left leg was poor, and the blood flow to that leg was further compromised by his being bedridden. Gangrene set in, and the doctors advised amputating the left leg.

My mother could not bring herself to let them mutilate him. It meant, however, that the infection would kill him.

I agreed with my mother.

His funeral was held in Waltham, the town where he was

born and raised. He was buried in Mt. Feake cemetery in Waltham. Because Dad loved being on the water in his boat, his headstone bears a carving of an outboard motorboat. Some of our finest family vacation memories revolve around the boat.

I don't remember crying, and now I wonder about that. I felt more relief than anything else — relief that he was not suffering anymore. But tears never came. It was too close to Lisa's death, and I had already closed down emotionally. Being widowed was not an experience I ever thought I would share with my mother.

⚓

The same week Dad died, my Uncle Walter died. My mother and her sister became widows the same week.

I remember visiting Uncle Walter during his illness. He was in Emerson Hospital, on the same floor where Lisa had been and in the room next to where she had passed away. It was eerie visiting him, only because of the close proximity to Lisa's room.

During my early years, ours had been a close-knit Italian family. All the brothers and sisters on my mother's side or my father's were always getting together, and as children, we went along to these family gatherings. When I was a teen-ager I had worked for my Uncle Walter. While in college I ate dinner at his house at least once a month.

So to visit him when he was in Emerson was not a choice but an obligation of love. He was family, and that mattered more than my grim memories of the place where Lisa died.

Ups And Downs

November 1997. Four years without Lisa. This is the first holiday season without my father, so the boys and I fly to Massachusetts to spend Thanksgiving with my mother.

I offer my mom a shoulder to cry on and an ear if she wants to talk about my father. It's been only six months since he died, and I know what it feels like. I know where I was at six months and realize I have come a long way since then. It feels so good to bring some joy into her life by having her grandsons around for Thanksgiving.

I am at peace about Dad's passing.

⚓

It's early December, and I go on a field trip with Victor's class — a walking tour of Old Naples. At lunch, some of the kids tickle Victor. Hearing him laugh and giggle warms my heart.

The first time I heard the boys laugh after Lisa died was delightful, yet I was saddened by the thought of what Lisa was missing. Today, I don't think of Lisa missing his laughter. I think of his laughter and how great it is to hear it. Now I'm aware that I don't think of Lisa missing out on our lives; she is just missing.

Four years is a long time to a ten-year-old, and to me, too. It's not that I'm forgetting her. It's more that she has not been part of our day-to-day life for those four years, and that's making my awareness of her lessen as time goes on. There is so much that needs to be attended to; I have to think about how I will do all these tasks instead of thinking about Lisa.

When she was alive, I thought of how to make her smile and laugh. She was alive, and my consciousness was alive with thoughts of her. Now I just have the memories. I can remember the day I met her, the time we spent together, and the day she died. I miss how we shared special events and precious moments in the kids' lives.

But her presence is fading.

The grief has subsided. During the past four years, parts of who I used to be keep popping back into my brain like a light bulb being turned on. Now I am feeling much more like my old self. I am more focused on my goals. It is part of the process of assimilating the new me, the new city, and the new life that I find myself living.

I know what I had and felt with Lisa, and I am looking for that again. Maybe I am searching too hard. Maybe I'm being too picky. I meet many women, yet I get tired of dating, and I don't find what I'm looking for in a woman. Lisa had that special spark. Surely, other women have it, too. I'm driving myself crazy. I go out by myself at times because it's easier. Sometimes I don't plan and wind up alone on the weekends.

The kids still ask if I will marry again. I tell them yes. They want a mom again, and I want them to have one. I want a wife again to share what I have — the love I want to give to the right woman.

⚓

Grief can be brought on by pieces of a song, old homes, or places we have been. The memories of our life, once traumatic to think about, are now pleasant thoughts, and I can smile at the memories. We had a good marriage. I did my best in loving her, and I felt her love in return.

On December 14, 1997, I don't grieve. I remember, and then get on with living. On the 15th, I keep the kids home from school so we can be together. On a scale of one to ten the day is a three. I show them a tape that Lisa and I had made — our anniversary tape. We would sit in front of the video camera and recount what had happened the previous year. We missed only the first two years because we didn't have a camera. We made the tapes so the kids would have an opportunity to see us and hear us, and hear about themselves, too. It is sad, but it is good to see Lisa looking so healthy.

⚓

Four years without Lisa is half the number of years we were married. Next year, Nick will have lived half his life without a mother. This year is my fifth Christmas without her. Four years ago it was very different.

Four years ago, I bought only a few gifts. The nurses at the hospital gave some to the kids. The boys opened their gifts with excitement. I couldn't. There was no gift that would give Lisa back to me. After the gift opening, I went upstairs and opened the bags from the hospital and put away her clothing. The memories were my present.

⚓

I no longer need the comfort of sleeping with Lisa's sweatshirt close to my chest like a toddler's security blanket. I still keep a sweater and a nightgown in the bottom drawer of my nightstand. They too have lost her presence, so I rarely look at them or touch them. Even with the memories, they are becoming just pieces of clothing. Although I feel that it's a waste to take up space with them, I am not ready to part with these objects.

In Massachusetts, I have a few items left that I look at from time to time, but the only piece I intend to keep is her wedding veil. I've grown beyond that. I'm more self-assured, more comfortable with my life as a single person.

Christmas in Florida is bright with lights, and we are excited by the reports of snow up north.

⚓

New Year's Day 1998 is here, and Nick and I have the flu. Steph makes dinner one evening, and Carl cooks the next night. On the third day, everyone waits for me to feed them. I have no appetite to cook, and I realize how dependent everyone is on me. How can I recharge my energy when needed?

I want to be the perfect dad, not the one who forgets things or gets stressed out. I've had it with the boys' laundry. I pick up the basket containing their dirty clothes and find clean, folded items underneath the dirty ones. I tell them they'll have to do their own laundry.

Being a single parent is tiring and stressful, yet I know it's just part of my journey. I feel some pride in accepting this.

⚓

I'm very frustrated. I have a new computer at work, and I can't figure out how to copy the files from the diskette to the hard drive. Writer's block overwhelms me today. I don't know what to write about, and I'm scared that I'm losing my creativity. I'm afraid my imagination is drying up, and that I'll want to become an accountant like my mother, brother, and sister. I'm lost and floating in time with nothing specific to do — no direction.

I feel all those old negative emotions creeping back because tomorrow would have been Lisa's 43rd birthday.

Most days I am able to concentrate on my writing. I haven't been published yet, but I feel my material is getting better, and I'm learning to use research effectively. I continue the weekly writing of the Kiwanis newsletter, and I write regularly in my role as Secretary on the Board of Trustees at the boys' school.

⚓

The ups and downs during the years without Lisa are having an impact on me. Forty-four sounds so old to me now. Some days I feel old, tired, and lacking direction. I fear my writing is going nowhere because it is garnering the typical rejection letters. That's part of this job. Where do I go to get positive feedback? Friends can give me only so much, but they aren't in my life all the time like a wife. Another painful twist: the person who bolstered my self-confidence the most isn't by my side to give me a boost when I need it.

I can't wait for the summer so I can get out of Florida and have time to relax and think. Sometimes I feel there are no women for me in Florida, and sometimes I think I can handle the women here. It's funny, sad, exciting, and frightening all at the same time.

Then I have a day like today when I'm able to step back and see the bigger picture. I know there are many lessons for me in Lisa's passing. I need to stand up and be counted, to make things happen instead of watching and waiting. I also have to find a way to believe in myself the way Lisa always believed in me.

Embracing Each Day

June 1998. Almost five years without Lisa. We return to Massachusetts for the summer. I decide to learn to fly, something I've wanted to master for years. I get information about flying lessons at the nearby Fitchburg Airport. My 20-minute introductory lesson is smooth and easy, and I enjoy the panoramic views from the plane. I make arrangements for my first lessons to be held Monday, Wednesday, and Friday next week.

On Monday, I get my first full-hour lesson. The flight instructor lets me take the controls, and I send us up, down, turning left, then right. Then I try a turn while going up, then another going down. My stomach betrays me, and I feel close to throwing up. I also get a headache.

I have to cancel the next two lessons because my head hurts and I'm nauseated. I know I get dizzy, but it is pretty bad when I have to spend a week to recover from my first flying lesson. By the end of the summer, I have five hours of flying and five shirts soaked with sweat.

We spend time at the lake, and I notice that Victor's voice sounds different. I attribute it to the lake water in his throat.

⚓

In September 1998 we are back in Florida for the start of another school year. Victor is in fifth grade, and Nick is in fourth.

Victor's voice has changed, and he has sprouted up. He is 11 and wears the same size shoes as I do. I notice how he sometimes looks at girls. I also see how they look at him. He is starting piano lessons again and Jiu-Jitsu. He also joined the junior varsity soccer team at school. This is surprising to me because he has never shown an interest in sports.

Nick wants to play soccer. He talks to the coach to try to get in the game, but he is too young.

I continue my flying lessons at the Naples Air Center. I'm still writing and dabbling in a new area — children's writing.

I start another term as Secretary of the Seacrest Board of Trustees. There is a possibility that I could be the Chairman of the Board some day. This is intriguing for me, and I realize I need to speak out more if I ever hope to be considered for that position.

⚓

Victor's soccer season is due to end after Halloween, and he mentions that basketball season will start in December. He wants to know if I would coach the junior varsity basketball team this year.

I am excited to think I could coach and lead a team. I haven't stepped out and done something like this before. However, I don't know that much about the rules of the game or even how to form a play. So I am excited and scared at the same time.

The P.E. teacher at Seacrest calls and asks if I want to coach basketball. I say yes. I am nervous about coaching because I don't know if the boys will accept me, or even if I can run a practice. My friend who works for the YMCA lends me the Y's book on coaching basketball. This is a big help because it explains about practices and team plans.

⚓

On Halloween, I take the boys to a Seacrest family's house, where other Seacrest parents and children are gathering. We walk around the neighborhood as the kids run from house to house. The boys want to sleep over at a friend's house, so I let them. It's Saturday night, and I have time to myself. I think about going out but decide to stay home. I call a couple of friends, but they're not home. So, with the lights low, I clean the kitchen counters, then I read, watch a little TV, and go to bed. It's such a blessing to have sleep come more naturally to me now.

Last month I had a free night, and I hated it. I felt a need to fill my time and my life. But now I feel comfortable enough with myself and my situation to stay home and feel good about it. I feel whole. I don't need someone to fill my time with. It's another piece of me that has come home, to be rediscovered and reclaimed. I feel great.

Basketball practice begins. The boys listen to me. They respect my authority because I am the coach. This is cool!

⚓

We arrive in Massachusetts for Thanksgiving with my mom, Carl, and my brothers. During the day we visit friends. The day after Thanksgiving, I take the boys to their first professional hockey game, and we watch the Boston Bruins defeat Montreal. They really enjoy it.

The next day we go shopping at Searstown Mall in Leominster. I have gift certificates for Walden Books, so we stop there first. As we leave the bookstore, I notice a Christmas tree sponsored by a local women's shelter. Each ornament on the tree bears the name of a woman and a suggested gift. The idea is to take a name, buy a present for the woman, then bring it back and place it under the tree. The shelter will distribute the gifts to women who would otherwise have nothing this Christmas.

Although the boys are reluctant, I pick a name off the tree. Victor and Nick don't have a mom to buy for; I don't have a wife to buy for. The least we can do is help someone else.

We go into the drug store to buy miscellaneous stuff for the woman in need. Nick picks out a pack of Tic-Tacs, a small snowman doll, and some aromatic soaps. Victor chooses some cheerful Christmas items. I select a card.

We bring the bag of goods to the mall's service desk. I open the card to sign it, and I just stare at it for a while. I want to write that my kids lost their mother, and that I've lost my wife. I want her to know the circumstance of loss we share. The emotions of my loss come flooding up, and I feel I am going to cry. I just can't write what I wanted to convey, so I sign it from "people who care."

⚓

When we arrive back in Florida, Nick asks, "Can we take December 14th off from school?"

"Let me think about it," I reply.

Nick is the one who reminds me of important dates, like the anniversary of his mom's death. I tell him we will do something special on that day, but they can't take the day off from school.

On one hand, it bothers me that I didn't think of Lisa's death in connection to the date. On the other hand, I'm glad I hadn't thought of it. The day is no longer traumatizing. It bothers me, though, that I may be forgetting her. Nick doesn't forget; he mentions his mom more often than Victor.

Nick and I talk about forgetting what she was like — the sound of her voice, her mannerisms, the way she walked. We do have videotapes showing these things. The videos were intended for Lisa and me to watch and remember what the kids were like when they were small. I never thought the boys and I would be watching them as a means to remind us what she was like.

The tapes show us how she moved, talked, laughed, and looked. What is lost is the way she touched us, how she smelled, and the feeling of love. The tapes give us a glimpse, but not enough of her.

Nick wants a mom, someone he can go to besides me. "When I get a mom," he predicts, "I'll probably call her Dad because I'm used to having just a dad."

I want the boys to have a mom also. I want a wife, someone to hold again, kiss, and keep close to my heart.

⚓

It is the fifth anniversary of Lisa's death. The boys and I go bowling and have lunch at my office. Sue, Joe, and I tell stories about Lisa.

"When your mother was pregnant with you, Victor," Sue remembers, "she thought she could still do everything the same as if she weren't pregnant." Sue described the time she carried heavy boxes and jumped off the loading dock, hurting her feet. Joe told the story of Miss V's hot sauce, a sauce so hot that a drop would do for a pot of stew. Lisa didn't believe it and put a teaspoonful in her mouth. The pain was evident on her face, and I could imagine smoke pouring from her ears. I told them about what she made me one year for Christmas: a whisker collector for trimming my mustache.

All of us were forgetting how she was on a day-to-day basis. I've accepted that this is normal and nothing to fear. Yet who she was, what she accomplished, and the things she did will never be forgotten.

At any time, I can still see in my mind's eye the first time we met, our first trip together to Bar Harbor, Maine, the house we bought in Wareham, skiing, pregnancies, and labor. I was fortunate, indeed, to have a love like hers.

⚓

It has now been five years in Florida. Life seems pretty normal. The boys have school, I have work, and we do homework and other stuff that families do. But not everything is good right now.

I'd quit my job if I had one. I'm frustrated with writing, and I have no personal life. The only constant is cleaning the kitchen. I'm behind in all my reading. I've discovered that I need a regular routine.

There is one high point: I flew my first solo around Naples Airport. It was a thrill and boosted my confidence.

As a writer I am stuck. I don't know what my voice is or my style. I feel uninspired and hopeless, unable to write fiction for children or adults.

My eyesight is adding to my frustration. I have trouble focusing, and I have to sit farther away from the computer screen. I feel as if my body is falling to pieces. I'm getting fat, and I have no social or sexual life.

I drive to Fort Lauderdale for the weekend to attend the Lifespring personal growth basic course. It is a "feel good" course that gives me a little insight into myself, but not much, so I enroll in the advanced class.

The advanced course is four days. I hate the digging deep within me to places that are hidden and painful. During a break I go to my hotel room, and a grief attack washes over me. I curl up on the bed. I want to reach out to someone. I want to be held and told everything will be all right. Will it be all right? I make it through the break.

At the end of the four days, I realize that I was beating myself up over Julia. I was telling myself that I was a piece of crap for not following through with my adoption commitment. I love Julia and did the best for her, and I don't need to carry that guilt anymore.

⚓

We continue through another basketball season. I encourage the boys, and they work hard. Everyone plays in the games, and everyone has a chance to start a game. We win our last game, and the kids are thrilled. I am too.

Nick's Little League baseball season has started. His coach doesn't speak well to the kids. He is disrespectful and belittling. After the game, we parents argue with the coach and among ourselves. His wife wants him to quit. I tell him we don't want him to quit, we just want him to talk differently to the kids. I am surprised that I am here because I usually avoid confrontations. But I am here, thanks to things I've learned through my self-improvement classes.

Now the coach likes me.

⚓

A friend once suggested that if I approach people as if I love them, I'll show people who I am. This thought stays with me as I clean the house for a dinner party. A group of parents from the school, whose kids are in an extracurricular program called Odyssey of the Mind, are getting together. I have known many of these parents for several years. We have been together during some of our children's most successful moments. We have become a close-knit group.

After they arrive, the kids are given a problem to work out while the grownups sit at the table and talk. My table is a rectangular, white wood-top table, covered with a sheet of glass. Under the glass I have family pictures.

As I get up from my chair, my eye glimpses a picture of Lisa. These people never met her, yet they know the kids. I feel it is time for them to meet her. I take the picture out and begin to tell my guests about Lisa. I tell them she was an incredible woman in every way. I share snippets from our years together. I even mention Julia, stop a moment, and take a breath. Yes, Julia was part of my life. I tell them how I decided to give her away. Everyone seems so grateful that I am opening up my heart. They gently ask questions, and I answer them freely.

Then I talk about Lisa's brave battle with cancer and her fight for life. What do I have to hide? I tell them about her discovery of a lump in her abdomen, which turned out to be a very rare form of cancer — carcinoma of the appendix. I talk about how she underwent her first surgery on her 35th birthday, and although she knew the tumors had spread, Lisa never gave up hope of a full recovery.

I tell them about getting a phone call and rushing to Emerson Hospital that December night in 1993. It all comes back as if it were yesterday. The past becomes the present, and I describe in detail those final days of Lisa's life.

> I enter Lisa's room and go to the left side of her bed. I take her hand in mine. Her breathing is steady as she inhales and exhales. Her wonderful blue eyes are wide open and staring at the ceiling.
>
> "Hi, hon," I say.
>
> She doesn't answer.
>
> I shift my face into her field of vision, but her eyes — cold and lifeless — don't move, twitch, or blink.
>
> A nurse brings a chair so I can sit close to Lisa. I hold her hand and talk to her. All day, nurses, friends, and family come by. In between visits I talk to Lisa about what was happening at home. I reminisce with her about our ski trips. I recall my proposal on the ski lift and how she didn't drop a thing when she opened the little ring box. I grin, recalling for her how I skied like a novice, falling and landing under a snow gun throwing out snow — this funny family story we were going to share with our grandkids.
>
> I doze for a while and awake to find moonlight stream-

ing in the window. At 10 p.m. a nurse brings a cot for me to sleep on. Why didn't I stay overnight before?

The next day my family members from out of town come to visit. I walk out into the hall with my brother Steve.

"How can you be so calm?" Steve asks as he struggles with his emotions.

"My time will come," I say. I don't know what I mean; I just know that right now I have to be strong.

My mom and dad are too bereft to speak, but their comforting hugs renew my strength. The first time Dad met Lisa, he told Mom he thought I should marry her.

Another day passes, and it is now Monday morning. Still in Lisa's room, I am reluctant to leave her side. I'm afraid she will die when I am not there. I have to be here. I can't explain it, but I must be here when she dies. The day we wed, I took a vow to be together "til death do us part." It's a vow I will never break.

The nurses have been great to Lisa. She had been one of them years ago, right in this very hospital. They check on me regularly and even bring me food. One of Lisa's doctors comes to the room to talk to me. I agree with him and sign a "do-not-resuscitate" order. Lisa would never want to be put on a life-support machine.

Around noon Lisa's breathing changes from the regular rhythm of the past three days to a ragged sound. I know this is not good.

In the early evening, Mrs. Niemi arrives. She is a spiritual counselor who became a good friend to Lisa and me before Lisa was first diagnosed. Mrs. Niemi and I stand beside the hospital bed, talking and praying. Gail comes to visit as the 11:00 p.m. nursing shift changes. Lisa's duty nurse ignores the shift change and stays in the room with us.

It is just past midnight, now Tuesday. Gail sits on Lisa's left side, and I am on the right. I caress Lisa's hand. Something has taken hold of me. I tell Lisa that if it is time for her spirit to go, to let it go in peace.

Words flow gently from my soul: "Let love surround you as you transition. I love you and release my love to go with you."

I don't want her to die but know she is dying. I don't want her to go, but I don't want her to suffer anymore either.

"I love you. Let love surround you." I watch her lips and feel I can see her breath. She inhales and exhales. "Let love surround you." She inhales and exhales.

"Go in peace," I whisper.

There is no inhale. Her lips are still.

⚓

My voice cracks slightly as I finish my story, and the men and women around the table dab at the tears in their eyes. Then I tell them I realize that in the past five years of my life without Lisa, I have come a long way. Before, when I thought of Lisa or admitted she was dead, I felt like I was drowning in a sea of sorrow. But not now. I am proud of who Lisa was and our love. I am proud of where I was in my journey through grief and how far I have come in assimilating her death into my life and making a new life. I know grief will still visit me from time to time, but I am alive, opening my heart, and life is good. I have emerged as a stronger person with a passion for living.

As I watch my boys interacting with the other kids — playing, talking, and laughing — it dawns on me that Victor and Nicholas really *did* save me! They gave me all the reasons in the world to keep on living and embrace each day.

Epilogue

Ten years without Lisa. The boys and I stroll through Coastland Center Mall in Naples, Florida. Victor is on my left, and Nick is on my right. As we walk, I look at the other people and families, and I glance at my boys. If people are behind us, they don't see a dad with two kids. They see three grown men. Sixteen-year-old Victor is six feet tall and has his driver's license. Fifteen-year-old Nick is 5'8" and has his learner's permit.

Carl, Lisa's dad, has been in a nursing home for the past three years. He gave me power of attorney so I can handle all his affairs. In the past ten years, I have received one letter from Lisa's older sister, Bonda.

Christmas is a joyous time, a time for remembering, for sadness, and renewal of life. It is the time of year I receive a card and a picture of Julia and her siblings. It is amazing to see her growth through the past ten years, and it comforts me to see her great smile.

Both boys attend Naples High School. Their career paths, as of today, are different, yet they both want to entertain people. They have not started dating, and I laugh at the thought that we could double-date.

Victor started playing the piano at age ten and still plays. He takes piano and guitar lessons. He played percussion instruments in a couple of Seacrest School's musicals. He and two of his friends have formed a band. They write original songs and will soon play their first show. He inspires me to try writing songs, a desire I have had for the past 30 years. He wrote a piano piece, and one section brings tears to my eyes. It hits a spot in me that reminds me of love and loss. It's an amazing connection.

He also played four years of basketball and soccer at Seacrest, played Little League and Junior League baseball, and studied the martial art of Jiu-Jitsu.

Nick is an athlete. He also played four years of soccer and basketball at Seacrest as well as four years of Little League baseball, and studied Jiu-Jitsu. He can execute forward flips with a twist and back flips on the trampoline in our backyard. He has been working at Dairy Queen, and in his own words, he is "a member of the fast food workers of America," so he appreciates how hard restaurant people work. His sense of humor is phenomenal.

Over the past five years I wrote the weekly Kiwanis newsletter, had two articles on fatherhood published in a local publication, and spoke to several school classes about both the process of writing and journalism as a career. I feel that my career is back on track.

I coached basketball at Seacrest for four years and served on the Board of Trustees of Seacrest School for six years. I didn't become Chairman, but that's okay; I think I served the school best by being Secretary. I learned how to fly airplanes, took ballroom dancing lessons, guitar lessons, studied Jiu-Jitsu, and learned to ride a motorcycle. I have dated the same woman for the past 10 months, which is the longest I've dated anyone. She is learning to cope with a man who still loves his deceased wife, and I am learning how to be romantic and caring again, which is not always easy for either of us.

I love to travel, and I take the boys with me so they can have fun and learn about the world. In 1996 I took the boys to Italy, a trip that was stressful but fun. We have been to Nashville, and Gatlinburg, TN, for fun and cave exploring, and I also took the boys to Atlanta for a weekend of baseball. In 1999 I took the boys and Carl to London and Sweden. The next year we all went to Cooperstown, NY, to visit the Baseball Hall of Fame and to explore Howe's Cavern.

We still have the house in Leominster, Massachusetts, which we've repainted and redecorated the last several years. It doesn't spark painful memories the way it did years ago. I know I will probably sell it soon, which will be traumatic, but necessary.

I talk to Lisa and my dad often. I tell Lisa what she is missing and thank her for the years of love and laughter that we shared. I also thank her for being such a great businesswoman and securing the financial future for me and the boys. I tell Dad what I am doing, that after 33 years of yearning, I finally got my own motorcycle.

In helping to spread the good that has come from life with Lisa, I donated money to Seacrest School to have the math challenge lab named after her. The plaque outside the door reads, "In memory of Lisa Ballo: wife, mother, and inventor." I also established the Melissa C. Johnson Nursing Scholarship at Florida Gulf Coast University and the Richard Ballo Journalism Scholarship at Suffolk University in Boston.

In memory of Lisa, I make regular charitable contributions to hospices because hospice bereavement support helped me and the boys through our early days of grief. I also donate to food banks because years ago when I was a struggling writer, I knew what it was like to be broke and hungry. For years I was angry at cancer and didn't want to donate money to any cancer organizations because I gave my wife to cancer. I have resolved that anger and now do what I can to support the local cancer fund.

⚓

One night I am paying bills in my home office. It's 11 p.m., and there is a knock on the door.

"Can I come in?" asks Nick. "Can we talk?"

"Sure, come on in." I wonder if he wants to talk about the wrestling team or continue the talk on sex I tried to have earlier.

"I've got a chip on my shoulder," he says.

I look up from my paperwork. On his shoulder sits a potato chip. He's smiling.

I laugh.

"This still makes me laugh," he says. "A chip on my shoulder."

"Let me see the chip," I say.

He hands me the chip and I pop it into my mouth.

"Is it stale?" asks Nick.

I munch it. "No."

"Good night, Dad."

"Good night, Nick."

As he walks away, I feel the all-familiar pang of grief. His sense of humor is exactly like his mom's. It reminds me of what I have lost. I know grief and I have survived it, and yet it still surprises me when it hits.

A chip on his shoulder, Nick said. I just have to laugh.

⚓

The boys and I are no longer adrift in a sea searching for something — anything — to hold onto. Our love for each other has been our constant anchor. We are part of the community. We are a family. We can travel and laugh together. We have survived by staying together, keeping a sense of humor, working on our grief with the help of hospice, and keeping Lisa's love alive by reminiscing often.

What have I learned during my years without Lisa? I learned about my ability to love and to let love go when needed. I learned the value of family, friends, and people who care, no matter what happens to you.

I learned about my strength to face life and to make tough decisions for the right reasons. I learned about the resiliency of kids. It's amazing how they live as kids, grieve a little, and then live again. I planned many trips for the kids' sake so they could have as normal a life as possible. When their mom was alive, we often traveled as a family. I have learned to love life.

I have learned to forgive myself for feeling angry at Lisa for dying; that's a normal reaction, grief counselors have told me, given the tragic circumstances. I have learned to let go of the guilt I carried for so long, beating myself up because I thought there was something else I could have done to save her.

I have come back to where I was before Lisa died but have become more confident, willing to stand up and lead, and less afraid of life. I feel happy I met her, honored to have married her, and blessed for the life she gave me and the boys. We have created a life without Lisa, yet she is only a heartfelt, love-filled memory away.

Hospice Can Help

If you or someone you know is bereaved, please consider contacting your local hospice. As author Richard Ballo found, even though his wife Lisa had not been cared for by hospice during the final phases of her terminal illness, most hospices offer free grief support programs to members of the community. Such programs often include children's workshops conducted at local schools and churches.

To locate a hospice near you:

In the U.S.:

Contact the National Hospice & Palliative Care Organization. Website: www.nhpco.org; phone: 703-837-1500.

In Canada:

Contact the Canadian Hospice Palliative Care Association. Website: www.chpca.net; phone 800-668-2785.

⚓

In addition to hospices, there are numerous other organizations offering free grief support in local communities, such as churches, social service agencies, hospitals, nursing homes, and funeral homes.

Acknowledgments

The first years of life without Lisa wouldn't have been bearable without support from my family. My mother helps me immensely by staying with the boys when needed and giving me advice when I ask for it. My sister Stephanie not only lived with us for a year but continues to live nearby, enriching our lives daily with her thoughtfulness. My brothers Steve and Ed remain actively involved in our lives as well. Each has something special and unique to offer my boys. Carl has always been there for us, and now that his health is slowly waning, we visit him in the nursing home to reassure him how much we care.

My friends have been a godsend. They kept my feelings of isolation to a minimum when we moved from Massachusetts to Florida, and I want to thank them all for keeping in touch and caring, especially Gail, Ted and Jean, Carol, Allan and Chris, Eileen and Chris, and Ray. Thanks, Ray, for pulling me out of the house on many occasions and getting me back into having a social life.

My sincere and heartfelt thanks to Virginie for her strength and maturity that kept us on course for the first 18 months. I don't know what I would have done without her.

My greatest blessing has been watching Victor and Nicholas develop into young men. I know that they are good, honest, kind, compassionate, fun-loving people; the kind of men I would choose as friends. Now that they are teens, I am learning to separate from them and encourage their independence.

I am grateful to my extended family at Seacrest Country Day School: the teachers, staff, and fellow parents. Seacrest not only offered the boys a quality education but also provided me with a close-knit community.

I appreciate the volunteer opportunities given to me by the fun group of people at the North Naples Kiwanis Club, which enabled me to rekindle my love of writing.

My partners and employees of the M.C. Johnson Co. are terrific people and dedicated friends who helped me get through my worst days and continue to be a source of comfort today.

Karla Wheeler and her dedicated staff at Quality of Life Publishing Co. have provided tireless support, expert editing, and the professionalism needed to finetune the early manuscript and guide it through the rigorous publishing process.

There are so many people who make a positive difference in our lives and support us in endless ways, and it would take another book to list them all. I may not have mentioned everyone here, but please know you are in my thoughts, and I thank you for being you.

— *Rich Ballo*
Naples, FL

Guide to Grief: How to Help
Someone Who Is Bereaved

Diana Jacks, PhD, a retired clinical psychologist and author of *Here to There, Grief to Peace* (published by Quality of Life Publishing Co.) believes *Life Without Lisa* can help not only those who are deeply bereaved but also friends and family members.

"There are a number of grief issues Rich Ballo deals with that are typically misunderstood by family and friends," says Dr. Jacks. "By reading *Life Without Lisa,* people will gain a better understanding of what a bereaved person is going through."

Dr. Jacks offers the following insights.

ANGER

Rich writes about his feelings of anger — at Lisa and at himself — throughout much of *Life Without Lisa*. "It's perfectly normal to be angry," Dr. Jacks points out. "On page 43 Rich admits how angry he is at Lisa and even says to her, 'You could have talked to me about the fact that you were dying.'" Anger directed toward the person who died, oneself, doctors, or others often lingers for months — even years, says Dr. Jacks.

HOW CAN YOU HELP? "Simply listen and validate that you understand the person is angry," she says. "You can't convince them not to be angry, but you *can* encourage the person in mourning to find healthy ways to vent the anger: punch a pillow, jog around the block, write a letter of anger and then burn it."

Other examples of anger occur on pages 31, 43, 64, 68, 71, 89-90, 125-126, and 133.

EASILY OVERWHELMED

There are many times in *Life Without Lisa* when Rich is easily overwhelmed by simple tasks or decisions. For instance, on pages 36 through 38, Rich tells about his inability to put together a television stand. When Lisa was alive he tackled much more challenging handyman jobs than assembling a store-bought piece of furniture. He chastises himself: "...I can't put together a stupid television stand without breaking down and crying."

Rich's ongoing struggles to complete tasks and make decisions are a common effect of grief, says Dr. Jacks. Shock waves from the death of someone dear often rob a person of their former abilities to function.

HOW CAN YOU HELP? "Be patient, give the bereaved all the time they need to regain their sense of self," notes Dr. Jacks. "Grief is a process, not an event." Rich explains what it feels like to be bereaved when he writes on page 38: "I feel like I have been hit on the head with a sledgehammer, yet I am supposed to act like nothing has happened and somehow keep on living a normal life."

Through the patient support of friends and family, Rich does eventually regain his self-confidence, notes Dr. Jacks, but he does so slowly, inch by inch, hour by hour.

Readers will find other examples of being easily overwhelmed and indecisive on pages 22, 36-38, 42, 48, 65, 71, 76, 131, 163, and 174-175.

GRIEF ATTACKS AND ANNIVERSARIES

On page 84 Rich tells how he broke down when hearing a song that reminded him of Lisa. Fortunately for Rich, he learned at his hospice grief support meeting that what he experienced was a grief attack, an acute upsurge of grief that can occur without warning. As Rich writes, "Anything can set me off. I feel like I'm walking through an emotional mine field."

HOW CAN YOU HELP? Reassure the person that their behavior is normal, given the depths of their grief. Share your knowledge about grief attacks and how they affected Rich. Suggest the person call a friend like you whenever a grief attack hits so they won't feel so alone and vulnerable. As Rich found, grief attacks often occur on important dates such as anniversaries. Be a good friend by anticipating such days whenever you can.

In her book, *Here to There, Grief to Peace,* Dr. Jacks calls this aspect of grief "Blind-Sided." Just when the bereaved thinks he has made great strides in the healing process, wham! A grief attack strikes. You can help by gently encouraging the bereaved to stay on their path of healing and not allow one blind-sided attack to derail them.

Dr. Jacks notes that in *Life Without Lisa,* we read that even 10 years after Lisa's death, Rich still has an occasional grief attack. "With time, such emotional waves become less frequent and much less severe," Dr. Jacks says. "Be a true friend by never responding in a judgmental way; always validate their pain and provide a safe haven for them to release some of their intense feelings."

Rich shares his grief attacks and anxiety over special holidays, birthdays, and anniversaries on pages 45, 84, 94-95, 97-98, 105, 117-118, 132-133, 137-139, 143-144, 145, 158, 166, 172-173, 180-181, and 182.

WHEN TO SHARE MEMORIES

On page 58, Rich relates a phone call he receives from a good friend who tries to be supportive. Rich writes, "I am not yet emotionally strong enough to listen to someone else sharing good memories of Lisa when I'm in the depths of sorrow." Yet earlier in his journal entries Rich writes that he wants to encourage family and friends to talk about Lisa.

HOW CAN YOU HELP? Knowing when it's appropriate to reminisce and when it might cause more pain for the bereaved can be challenging. "Let the person guide you," suggests Dr. Jacks. "If you begin to share a memory of the deceased but are unsure whether to continue talking, simply ask the bereaved person. You might say, "I have such warm memories of Lisa. Do you want me to share them now, or would another time be better?" Even if the person isn't comfortable answering you directly, you will learn to take certain cues from their voice or body language, which will help you to tune into their present state of mind and emotional neediness.

Other examples of sharing memories occur on pages 46, 70, 113-114, 120, 121-122, 134-135, 141, and 180-181.

SEPARATING FROM PERSONAL ITEMS

Dr. Jacks emphasizes, "I wish every friend or family member of a person in grief could read *Life Without Lisa* so they'd learn to keep their mouths shut." Dr. Jacks is referring to the fact that it took Rich almost three years to finally be ready to give away Lisa's clothes, purses, and other personal items. He was fortunate because his family and friends didn't nag him about sorting through and getting rid of her belongings.

"There is no magic timetable for parting with personal items," stresses Dr. Jacks. "Many well-intentioned people urge the bereaved to get rid of the deceased's belongings, thinking this will help speed up the grief process."

The opposite is often true, says Dr. Jacks. "By putting pressure on someone to say goodbye to precious belongings before they are emotionally ready for such separation often hinders the person's healing."

On pages 100 through 102, five months after Lisa's death, Rich decides to go through Lisa's things. He writes, "I reach my arms around the clothes and hug them, enveloping myself in the scent that still, even faintly, lingers in each fiber. If I get rid of her belongings, I would be getting rid of her, and I can't do that... Yet I believe I must start removing the signs of her life. I must move on and return to the person I was before, yet treasure the experience of being married to Lisa."

HOW CAN YOU HELP? Let the bereaved set the timetable and swallow your urge to nag them into removing personal belongings prematurely. By doing so, the bereaved will work it out in their own way, just like Rich did. Fifteen months after her death (page 150), Rich tries once again to sort through her things, but he knows he still isn't ready. It's too emotional, too final.

Then two and a half years after her death (page 160), Rich knows he is ready to part with her clothes. He cleans out her closets and takes a carload of clothes to a local charity that helps women get back into the work force. He writes, "...I finally understand that I don't want to become attached to symbols or make a memorial to her with her things. Her memory is alive within my mind and heart."

Rich writes about many aspects of separating from tangible aspects of Lisa, from parting with her clothes to redecorating the house and taking off his wedding band. Readers will find examples on pages 58, 87, 100-103, 107-109, 122-123, 124, 151-152, 154, 156, 159-160, and 173-174.

TALKING WITH CHILDREN

The way Rich communicated so openly with his young sons sets an excellent example for others to follow, according to Dr. Jacks. Right from the day after Lisa died, Rich chose to get them involved. On pages 15-16 we read that Rich takes his young sons with him to pick out a headstone. He writes, "The boys should not be shopping for a headstone at ages 5 and 6. But I want the boys to be part of the process because we are a family, and they need to feel involved."

Rich also allowed his sons to make their own decision about whether or not to attend the memorial service, which was an excellent thing to do, according to Dr. Jacks. "Because children grieve differently from adults, it's important to keep them involved but also give them space to opt out of some of the funeral activities."

HOW CAN YOU HELP? When a death affects young children, it's best to communicate with them openly, honestly, using clear words that come from the heart, notes Dr. Jacks. It's also important to reminisce about the person who died whenever a child seems ready to do so.

Dr. Jacks believes Rich sets a fine example throughout the book in the way he makes a point of sharing memories about Lisa with the boys, keeping alive certain family traditions with them, yet being open to creating new rituals as they continue on their healing journey of life without Lisa.

Examples of interactions with the children appear on pages 11, 15, 18, 20, 46, 55-56, 62, 70, 96, 123, 132-133, and 179-180.

INTIMACY ISSUES

Dr. Jacks believes Rich's openness about his struggles with intimacy after Lisa's death will help many readers. "There are many types of love," says Dr. Jacks, "and we grieve our losses on different levels depending on the depth of our relationship. When the person who died was a spouse or significant other, the loss of intimacy in itself can seem unbearable."

On page 91, four months after Lisa's death, Rich describes how he handles his first sexual urges since the loss of his soulmate and lover. Then on page 93, he admits how needy he is, yet he realizes he wants physical closeness with a woman but has nothing to give in return.

HOW CAN YOU HELP? Again, let the bereaved lead the way, suggests Dr. Jacks. Don't be pushy about lining up blind dates or forcing a person to begin dating again if they're not emotionally ready. As Rich says, "dating usually leads to intimacy, and even now — ten years after Lisa's death — I still sometimes struggle with intimacy."

Dr. Jacks emphasizes that intimacy issues can linger for a long time. "Be gentle with yourself," she concludes.

Rich reveals his vulnerabilities about dating and intimacy on pages 57, 69-70, 86, 91-94, 109-112, 119, 143-144, 147-148, 149-150, 152, 159, 161, 167, 172, and 175.

About the Author

Richard (Rich) Ballo lives in Naples, Florida, with his sons, Victor and Nick. While this is his first published book, he is working on several other book projects, both nonfiction and fiction.

When Rich and Lisa married, Rich was a successful technical writer. After the boys were born, he left his position to be a stay-at-home dad. He kept his journalism career alive by writing feature articles for their local newspaper. But after Lisa died, writer's block overwhelmed him, threatening to smother him in a blanket of frustration and failure. Little did he know that the journal he had been diligently writing would transform his insights into a journey that enlightens and assists others with the grieving process.

It is with humility and gratitude that Rich invites you to experience *Life Without Lisa*. He welcomes correspondence through his publisher:

Email: richballo@QoLpublishing.com

Mail: Quality of Life Publishing Co.
                  Attention: Rich Ballo
                  P.O. Box 112050
                  Naples, FL 34108-1929

THE HAPPY FAMILY. Above, left: *On vacation at Mt. Washington, New Hampshire, in 1991, the summer after Lisa was diagnosed with cancer. Left to right: Rich, Victor, Nick, and Lisa.* **Above, right:** *A family portrait taken later that year. Clockwise: Lisa, Rich, Victor, and Nick.*

MOMENTS WITH MOM. Above: *In January 1993, Victor (left) and Nick celebrate their Mom's 38th — and last — birthday.* **Right:** *Eight months later, Lisa poses with (left to right) Nick, Julia, and Victor.*

LIFE WITHOUT LISA. Above: *Lisa's lighthouse headstone.* **Left:** *ten years after Lisa's death, Nick, Rich, and Victor celebrate Nick's graduation from 8th Grade.*

How to Order

Quality of Life Publishing Co. specializes in gentle grief support books and booklets for readers of all ages. Here's how to order *Life Without Lisa* and other publications:

ONLINE: **www.QoLpublishing.com**
Purchase online using your Visa, MasterCard, Discover, or American Express card.

EMAIL: **books@QoLpublishing.com**

PHONE: **1-877-513-0099**
Toll-free in the U.S. and Canada
or call 1-239-513-9907

FAX: **1-239-513-0088**

MAIL: **Quality of Life Publishing Co.**
P.O. Box 112050
Naples, FL 34108-1929

*DISCOUNTS. Be sure to ask about **substantial discounts** available to hospices and other grief support organizations.*